DATE DUE

Google

SPEAKS

Google

—— SPEAKS ——

**Secrets of the World's Greatest
Billionaire Entrepreneurs,
Sergey Brin and Larry Page**

JANET LOWE

WILEY

John Wiley & Sons, Inc.

Published by John Wiley & Sons, Inc., Hoboken, New Jersey.
Published simultaneously in Canada.

For general information on our other products and services or for technical support, please contact our Customer Care Department within the United States at (800) 762-2974, outside the United States at (317) 572-3993 or fax (317) 572-4002.

Wiley also publishes its books in a variety of electronic formats. Some content that appears in print may not be available in electronic books. For more information about Wiley products, visit our web site at www.wiley.com.

Library of Congress Cataloging-in-Publication Data:

Lowe, Janet.
   Google speaks : secrets of the world's greatest billionaire entrepreneurs, Sergey Brin and Larry Page / Janet Lowe.
       p.   cm.
   Includes bibliographical references.
   ISBN 978-0-470-39854-8 (cloth)
      1. Brin, Sergey, 1973–   2. Page, Larry, 1973–   3. Computer programmers—United States—Biography.   4. Businesspeople—United States—Biography.   5. Internet programming—United States.
6. Google (Firm)   7. Google.   8. Web search engines.   I. Title.
QA76.2.A2L69   2009
005.1092—dc22
[B]
                                                                    2009004121

Printed in the United States of America

10 9 8 7 6 5 4 3 2 1

Dedicated to Stephen Plaxe, Carolyn Muller,
Audrey Sniegowski, Dale and Kathy Lowe,
Jade Easton, and all my other Angels.
Thank you.

Contents

Acknowledgments   xiii

INTRODUCTION   1

THE GOOGLE GUYS   13
  Sergey Brin   13
    Russian Roots   13
    American Passage   14
    Educating Sergey   15
    The Road to Stanford   15
    Boy Genius to Adult Genius   16
    Wedding on a Caribbean Sand Bar   17
    23andMe   18
    Flying High   20
  Larry Page   21
    Cradled in a Computer Culture   22
    Nikola Tesla, Page's Hero   23
    Tesla's Story   24
    The Tesla Car   25

Motivated by Montessori 26
The Leadership Program 27
The Solar Racer 28
Go West, Larry 28
Lego-centricity 29
Mensa Boy 30
Larry Gets Married 30
The X-Prize 31
No More Laundry 32
The Power of Partnership 33
Forging the Stanford Connection 35
A Creative Environment 35
A Poignant History 37
An Academic or an Entrepreneur? 39
A Grim Goodbye 39
Networking at Its Best 40
Burning Man 42

ADULT SUPERVISION **44**
The Collective Wisdom of Silicon Valley 45
He's Been the Rock; They've Been the Rockets 46
A Man of Influence 47
Climbing a Different Kind of Mountain 50

IN THE BEGINNING **51**
The Ultimate Search Engine 55
Not Inventing, but Improving Upon 57
Look Around You for Inspiration 59
How Search Works 60
Platform Power 63
Open Platform 66

GOOGLE BY ANY OTHER NAME — **68**

A Blessed Blunder — 68

From Noun to Verb — 69

Playing with the Name — 70

The Google Logo — 71

The Google Doodle — 72

Google Zeitgeist — 74

A COMPANY IS BORN — **78**

Yahoo! Drew the Map — 79

The Requisite Garage — 81

The Venture Capitalists — 83

The Elusive Business Plan — 86

Investing in Wild Ideas — 88

Good Ideas Put to Good Use — 91

Dealing with Dark Matter — 91

Aversion to Advertising — 93

Advertising that Delivers Results — 95

Two Ways to Advertise:
   AdWords and AdSense — 96

Extending the Google Reach — 100

The Science of Advertising — 101

Google Didn't Advertise Itself—at First — 101

Birth of the Google Economy — 104

GOING PUBLIC — **106**

"We're Different" — 109

The Dutch Auction — 111

Buffett on Google — 113

Berkshire Hathaway's Share
   Structure versus Google's — 114

The *Playboy* Interview   116
Ten Years Later   118

THE VISION   **123**
Make It Useful   125
   The Many Ways to Google   127
Make It Big   132
   We Serve the World   133
Make It Fun   135
   Google Users Hearken to the Call   138
Don't Do Evil   139
   How Google Defines *Evil*   140
   The Motto Loses Some Shine   143
   Can Free Speech Go Too Far?   144
Make It Free   146

GOOGLE CULTURE   **148**
New Management Style   149
Ten Things Google Has Found to Be True   153
Riding the Long Tail   156
20 Percent Projects   157
Perpetual Beta   159
Fabled Workplace   160
An Alternative Point of View   163
Googleplex   164
Google in Ireland   168
Top Ten Reasons to Work at Google   169
The Battle for Brainpower   171
Guarding the Secrets   177

GOOGLE GROWS UP   **180**
  Conflicts and Controversy   181
    Click Fraud   182
    Avoiding—or Not Avoiding—Pornography   184
  Privacy Issue   188
  Advertising Products   190
  Gmail   192
  Street View   193
  Can They Snoop—and Will They Tell?   197
  Hello, Human Rights   200
  The Great Chinese Firewall   201
  Principles of Freedom   203
  Copyright Infringement   205
  The Authors' Revolt   205
    Grand Ambitions   206
    The Snippet Defense   208
    Whose Property Is It, Anyway?   209
    All About Advertising   209
  The Game-Changing Settlement   210
  Lawsuits Everywhere   212
  Google Gets an Airplane   218
  Google Gets a Satellite   220

GOOD CITIZEN GOOGLE   **223**
  Google.org—the Philanthropic Part   225
  Google and the Environment   227
  Renewable Energy Less than Coal   229
  Geothermal Power   230
  Energy from the Sea   230
  Energy-Efficient Googleplex   231

GOOGLE'S FUTURE 233
Artificial Intelligence 238
Onward to Web 3.0 241
Cloud Computing 243
YouTube 248
The Google Phone 250
White Spaces 254

THE DOMINANT POWER IN THE INDUSTRY? 259
Google, Microsoft, and the Internet Civil War 264
The Battle of Yahoo! 267
Gates on Google 271

CONCLUSION 273
Lessons from Larry and Sergey 278
The Traits of Those Who Change the World 279

Timeline 281
Glossary 288
Notes 295
Permissions 315

– Acknowledgments –

Thank you to the following people for the enormous credit they deserve for this book: Joan O'Neil, Kevin Commins, Emilie Herman, and Mary Daniello at John Wiley & Sons, the staff at Cape Cod Compositors, my literary representative Alice Martell, copy and content editor Lynne Carrier, and advisors and helpers Alan Bradford, Jack Brandais, Warren Buffett, Ben and Carol DeBolt, Trudy Jenzer, John McDermott, and Professor Joel West.

Google

——— SPEAKS ———

Introduction

At the tenth birthday of Google Inc., founders Larry Page and Sergey Brin stood on the grounds of Vandenberg Air Force Base in central California. They watched in wonder as a state-of-the-art Delta 2 rocket blasted into the atmosphere, carrying a GeoEye-1 satellite into orbit. The satellite, adorned with the Google logo, would send back razor-sharp photos to be used in the company's popular mapping service.[1] What a glorious way to celebrate the first decade of a company that itself took off like a rocket from its very beginning.

Chris Winfield, who heads the search-engine ad firm 10e20, noted that in a very short time, Google has become a rage, the equivalent of the Beatles during the 1960s. "It's pretty amazing, it's almost like they are in control of the world."[2]

The story of the search-engine company Google and its two young founders is loaded with superlatives, secrets, and surprises. One thing is certain: The Google guys, Larry and Sergey, both now 36, have become the undisputed "lords of all information."[3]

In 2006, *Time* magazine called Google the "smartest company of the year" and one of the century's most game-changing enterprises. Google was crowned the world's largest search engine and one of the best-known global brands. Praise like that could well go to a company leader's head.

The Google founders have been described in many ways, including the *Thomas Edisons of the Internet*. Brin and Page are the twin Princes of High Technology who pulled the proverbial sword from the stone. They were groomed for greatness in the computer field from infancy; they traveled to a holy land (Stanford University and Silicon Valley) to prove their mettle in battle. They slew a whole den of dragons and emerged from the quest with flags of victory flying. Their story is a classic hero's journey.

Larry and Sergey were accustomed to the role of high achievers. Both are sons of scientists, and both grew up in technology-oriented households. Both were bright and accomplished in school. At Stanford and in Silicon Valley, they were surrounded by a court who knew the landscape of that charmed kingdom. Their professors were among the best in the field of computer science. His brother had already set up a company by the time

Larry enrolled at Stanford University, and the brother later sold it to Yahoo!. Sergey's father-in-law is a Stanford physics professor. His sister-in-law was a Silicon Valley venture capitalist.

Clearly, both men were exceptionally smart and had entrepreneurial personalities—and it was as if they quickly recognized the potential mirrored in one another. They followed their destiny when they developed Google search software. And the community around them, ever alert to the next big idea from techies just barely of legal age, was just waiting for them to step up.

To say Sergey and Larry were trained from birth for what they became does not diminish the vast importance or meaning of what they have done. In the 12 years since they first began collaborating on a graduate school project, the Google guys have:

- Started a business in a college dorm room with no more assets than a great idea.
- Built the largest index of Web pages in the world. Google catalogued its trillionth Web page in the summer of 2008.
- Launched with $100,000 private capital and developed into a public corporation with a market capitalization of around $100 million.
- Expanded from just the two of them to more than 20,000 employees.

- Grown their company into a giant with a 1.5-million-square-foot headquarters in Mountain View, California, plus two dozen other U.S. offices and technical centers in more than 30 countries.
- Gathered a customer base, starting with those using a college website and becoming one of the most global corporations in existence.
- Spread from a single service to a Web portal with dozens of services and products
- Dominated the Internet search industry, handling more than 70 percent of all U.S. searches.
- Developed advertising revenues of around $16 billion a year. This is nearly as much advertising revenue as generated by the four major TV networks combined.

Sergey and Larry were ranked as numbers 32 and 33 on *Forbes'* 2008 list of billionaires, with each of them worth more than $18 billion at the time. They subsequently lost about $6 billion in the value of their Google stock, but they remained fabulously rich.

With their fortune came fame. Not so many years after Google debuted, Larry and Sergey visited an Israeli high school for gifted math students. When the pair walked on the stage in the auditorium, they were greeted with a roar usually reserved for rock stars. "Every student there, many of them immigrants like Sergey from the former Soviet Union, knew of Google."[4] And like budding scientists everywhere, many of the students hoped to achieve the same success and status.

Despite a distinct nerdiness, their regal demeanors have shown forth in the way they initially marketed their company, as they dealt with venture capitalists, in the way they chose a chief executive officer, in the path by which they took Google public, and later, when dealing with contentious issues such as corporate secrecy, privacy, the intellectual property of others, corporate governance, and new product development. They invariably acted independently and with self-assurance, if not with a good dose of divine right.

"There has never been a company," wrote author Ken Auletta, "whose influence extended so far over the media landscape, and which had the ability to disrupt so many existing business models."[5]

To survive the economic downturn, Google has hunkered down, prioritizing investments in display advertising, online business software, and mobile telephone ads. Nevertheless, the company remains robust.

Page and Brin have become about as powerful as it is possible to be in the high-tech industry. And they have been able to spin that power up to a global level. In Great Britain, the newspaper *The Guardian* publishes the *MediaGuardian 100* list, ranking the most powerful individuals in media. The roll embraces every sector, including print news, broadcasting, publishing, advertising, and digital media. Larry and Sergey took the top slot. Microsoft's Steve Ballmer was seventh on the list. Yahoo's Jerry Yang, who just months before was a Silicon Valley celebrity entrepreneur, was not to be found

In order to expand their audience, potential targets for advertising, Google has come up with an astounding array of products. These include an online classified advertising site, a project to scan every book ever published and put excerpts on line, e-mail, instant messaging service, mobile phone software, and so on. Google also sells content, for example, via an online video store selling TV shows and National Basketball Association games.

It's easy to think of advertising simply as an economic activity, albeit a somewhat annoying one to many consumers. But advertising is clearly more than that. "You can tell the ideals of a nation by its advertising," wrote travel writer Norman Douglas in 1917.[6]

~

Even though Google management is locked in on advertising profits, there is time for fun. Google gets a little whimsical with such dreams as building a space elevator that can deliver goods to the moon. Google is more than a place to sneak in a vanity search, learn more about a blind date, or click on ads.

Larry Page and Sergey Brin have been the cutting edge of Internet search and have managed their leading positions superbly. Even more intriguing is their involvement in so many other front-running technologies. They played a role in four of *Time* magazine's best inventions, including the first and second. First place went to 23andMe, a genetic testing company cofounded by Sergey's wife, Anne; number two was the Tesla green sports car; and forty-ninth was Nanosolar, a solar energy company producing a thin, lightweight, affordable solar panel. Larry and Sergey were early investors in all three companies, and Google itself has invested in 23andMe. The fourth-ranked great invention of 2008 was Google's own idea, wind-powered computer data centers.

Google has thousands of engineers working on innovative applications for Internet and mobile use. They also are collaborating with the National Aeronautics and Space Administration (NASA) to build a high-technology campus at Moffett Field near Google headquarters. Under a 40-year agreement, Google will lease 42.2 acres of bare land from NASA to construct up to 1.2 million square feet of offices and research and development (R&D) facilities.[7]

Google and NASA have begun collaboration on several projects, including one that makes it easier for the scientists to publish planetary data on the Internet. The project has already provided high-resolution lunar imagery and maps to the Google Moon program and resulted in the "NASA" layer in Google Earth. Similarly, the Global Connection project enhances the "National Geographic" layer in Google Earth by embedding geo-referenced stories and images from around the world. The Disaster Response project develops prototype software tools to help improve first response to large-scale natural disasters.

Even the Pentagon sought Google's advice on how better to manage information technology.[8]

~

The founders themselves are generally considered to be good guys, well-intentioned and doing their best. In their bachelor days they engaged in what seems like innocent fun. One photo on the web shows Sergey at a fraternity party dressed as a girl.[9]

Google is an impressive introduction to the twenty-first century. By logging on to Google.com or one of its numerous other domains, you can locate information in dozens of languages, check real-time stock prices, find phone books for every U.S. city, get directions to your doctor's office, or even check out an aerial or street view of your own house.

This company takes us right into the borderless global society. Airplanes and telephones moved us in that direction; computers are speeding us ever closer. It's also a society that pushes for change, sometimes recklessly.

Nevertheless, change is inevitable, and Google is forcing governments to come up with new equitable guidelines and rules for the Internet milieu.

Google has a mysterious mojo that isn't easy to explain. Each of the 2008 U.S. presidential candidates trooped to Mountain View to meet with Google and Google employees. Andrew Orlowski, executive editor of the technology website, The Register, claims, "The Web is a secular religion at the moment and politicians go to pray at events like the Google Zeitgeist conference. Any politician who wants to brand himself as a forward-looking person will get himself photographed with the Google boys."[10]

Google set off a buzz at both the 2008 Republican and Democrat national conventions. The company sponsored centers for bloggers to report on their observations and insights at both meetings. At the Democratic convention in Denver, Colorado, the bloggers' headquarters was a two-story, 8,000-square-foot facility. Republicans had a similar setup in St. Paul, and more than 200 bloggers registered for credentials there. For the first time since the American Revolution, the potential existed for nontraditional, often nonprofessional, reporters to control breaking political news.[11]

Google's chief executive officer, Eric Schmidt, became an advisor to President Barack Obama's transition team, helping to choose cabinet members for the economy and technology. Additionally, the company has used its huge profits and influence to lobby Congress for advantageous regulatory changes and to compete in new fields, including software, wireless communications, and alternative energy sources.

Google's positive image began to shift as the company grew. At first, Google was the miracle of the twenty-first century; now, gradually it's beginning to be seen as a menace. In 2004, *Wired* magazine plastered pictures of Sergey and Larry on its cover above the title "Googlemania." Two years later, it ran another story, headlined "Googlephobia: Who's Afraid of Sergey? (Who Isn't?)."

As for this quick switch in attitudes, "I find it surprising," said Sergey.[12]

Nevertheless, even as the negative noise grew, Google customer satisfaction remained high. One rating service gave Google a score of 86 out of a possible 100. Apple scored one point below Google. By comparison, many U.S. airlines ranked somewhere between 54 and 62.[13]

~

Among the questions asked in this book are:

- What does it mean when a single company becomes our primary portal to the entire World Wide Web?

Almost overnight, Internet search became the most important tool for finding and processing information. Google has been extremely clever in finding new ways and new information to search. It also has gone beyond search with a Web browser, e-mail and other services.

- Should individuals be concerned about their privacy in relation to Google or other search engines? What steps can people take to protect themselves?
- Who owns intellectual property, and who is entitled to use the music, books, art, and other creations to earn money?
- Has Google become too powerful?
- What lies ahead for the company as it matures? Google is just over a decade old, after all. Larry and Sergey always need to be looking behind them, ready for the next youthful entrepreneurs who may be gaining on them.

~

Here are some tips for getting the most out of this book. Remember that Google comes out with advances, new products, and ideas with such speed that it's almost impossible to keep up. For that reason, this book focuses somewhat more on the company and the personalities who created and run Google than its technology.

The book is largely based on the words of Larry Page, Sergey Brin, Eric Schmidt, and others at Google. I've also included comments of those who follow the company closely. Thus the title: *Google Speaks*.

To keep track of the evolution of events at Google, turn to the timeline at the back of the book. To better understand the unique language of the Internet, refer to the glossary.

Finally, enjoy the book. The saga of Google is one of the most remarkable business tales ever told. Google has a lot to tell us.

The Google Guys

SERGEY BRIN

"Sergey was a good boy," his father joked, "when he was asleep."[1]

~

Russian Roots

Sergey Mikhailovich Brin is the son of a University of Maryland applied probability and statistics professor (his dad) and a NASA scientist (his mom). He was born in Moscow, Russia, on August 21, 1973. Sergey's parents fled to the United States when he was 6 years old, and by the time he was 21 he was on his way to becoming a multicultural marvel.

In Moscow, the family, including the parents and Sergey's grandmother, lived in a crowded 350-square-foot apartment. Sergey's toddler playground was a grim courtyard, where the boy spent two hours a day playing, regardless of how cold the weather.[2] Additionally, the family met with anti-Semitism in the streets and in the workplace. The outlook was so discouraging that the family knew they must leave.

When Sergey was 17, they returned to Russia for a visit, despite their nervousness at the reception they might receive. After Sergey saw the crumbling infrastructure and bleak atmosphere of his native Moscow, he felt grateful that his parents had immigrated.[3]

"I think, if anything, I feel like I have gotten a gift by being in the States rather than growing up in Russia . . . it just makes me appreciate my life that much more."[4]

American Passage

The family, including parents, grandmother, and young Sergey, landed in America on October 25, 1979. With the help of the Jewish community that sponsored them, Michael and Eugenia Brin found work suitable to their education and settled into a new life in Maryland, just on the perimeter of Washington, D.C.

The Brins had not lived a particularly Jewish-centered life in Russia. "We felt our Jewishness in different ways," explained Michael, "not by keeping kosher or going to synagogue. It is genetic. We were not very religious.

My wife does not eat on Yom Kippur. I do. We always have a Passover dinner. We have a Seder. I have the recipe for gefilte fish from my grandmother."[5]

Educating Sergey

For a while, young Sergey attended the Miskan Torah Hebrew School, but he didn't like it and after a few years stopped going.

Sergey was enrolled in the Paint Branch Montessori School in Adelphi, Maryland. He spoke English with a heavy accent when he entered the school. He didn't pick up language as quickly as the family hoped, but the bright-eyed, shy boy did adjust. His Montessori teacher, Patty Barshay, recalls, "Sergey wasn't a particularly out-going child, but he always had the self-confidence to pursue what he had his mind on."[6]

His father gave him a Commodore 64 computer when Sergey was 9. By middle school, Sergey was recognized as a math prodigy. He went on to Eleanor Roosevelt High School in Greenbelt, Maryland, where, according to some accounts, he was cocky about his math skills, often challenging teachers on their methods and results.

"I didn't systematically teach Sergey; he would ask when he wanted to know something," his father recalled.[7]

The Road to Stanford

You might say Sergey went to high school, college, and graduate school at the University of Maryland. He began studying math at the college when he was 15, and quit high school altogether after his junior year to enroll full time and graduated in three years.

After winning a National Science Foundation scholarship, Sergey applied to several graduate schools. Being rejected by MIT wasn't such a disappointment, since he had his heart set on going to California to attend Stanford. That school appealed to him because of its proximity to Silicon Valley and the nearby army of supportive high-tech entrepreneurs. Sergey headed west to earn his Ph.D.

He also welcomed the prospect of great weather. In California, Sergey easily took to campus social life, including skiing, rollerblading, and gymnastics.

When his father asked whether he was taking any advanced classes, Sergey replied, "Yes, advanced swimming."[8]

Rajeev Motwani, one of Sergey's advisors, remembers, "He was a brash young man. But he was so smart. It just oozed out of him."[9]

(*Note:* There is more on Brin's Stanford experience in the section "Forging the Stanford Connection.")

Boy Genius to Adult Genius

As an adult, Sergey is restless and edgy. His boyish good looks and low, sloping shoulders make him seem perpetually relaxed. He is active, studying the flying trapeze at a circus school in San Francisco (except that he fell and hurt his back) and practicing springboard diving. His puckish sense of humor often grabs people off guard, and at times even comes across as juvenile. Nevertheless, his Levi's, faded t-shirt, and crocs with socks or rollerblades are a cover for a purposeful, serious, even aggressive personality. Both Sergey and Larry are notorious workaholics.

Sergey still speaks with a slight Russian accent and ends many sentences with "and what not." Like Eric Schmidt and Larry Page, he overuses the word *scale*. Often, *scale* describes something that remains workable as it grows bigger, but in Googlespeak, it has come to mean something that can be developed into a profitable product.

Wedding on a Caribbean Sand Bar

It seemed curious that Sergey missed Google's 2007 Annual meeting, but then, the story came out that may have explained it. He was getting married.

Sergey's mother once expressed the hope that he would wed a "nice Jewish girl," and her wish came true. He married Anne Wojcicki in May 2007, in the Bahamas. Anne's great-grandfather on her mother's side was a prominent Russian rabbi who came to the United States in the 1920s.

With the bride wearing a white bathing suit and the groom wearing a black one, Brin and his longtime girlfriend swam to a sandbar, where a friend performed the nuptials.

Anne, a former health-care analyst turned entrepreneur, is the sister of early Google executive Susan Wojcicki. The sisters grew up in Palo Alto, where their father is the head of the physics department at Stanford. Their mother is a respected journalism teacher across the street at Palo Alto High School. Anne attended Yale University, graduating in 1996 with a degree in biology. Like Sergey, she is high-energy and athletic. She was a member of her college ice hockey team and a competitive ice skater.

Sergey and Anne became parents for the first time in the winter of 2008 with the arrival of son Benji.

23andMe

Google put $3.9 million into Anne Wojcicki's biotech startup, 23andMe. The company is built on the concept of individualized genetic mapping. Its name refers to the number of paired chromosomes in human DNA. Anne's company can tell you about your genetic origins, your propensity or resistance to certain diseases, and scores of other intimate details.

After submitting to genetic testing by 23andMe, Brin learned that he has a propensity for Parkinson's disease, a condition that affects his mother. In his blog, Sergey wrote:

This leaves me in a rather unique position. I now have the opportunity to adjust my life to reduce those odds. I also have the opportunity to perform and support research into the disease long before it may affect me.

He added, "I feel fortunate to be in this position."[10]

Until the fountain of youth is discovered, all of us will have some conditions in our old age, only we don't know what they will be. I have a better guess than almost anyone else for what ills may be mine and I have decades to prepare for it.[11]

Brin, along with his parents, contributed $1.5 million to the University of Maryland's Parkinson's disease research project.[12] And he also is involved with the Michael J. Fox Foundation.

Anne Brin appeared on the Oprah Winfrey show and talked about her pregnancy and the baby. "I looked at Sergey's profile and I looked at me, and we saw that the child has a fifty percent [chance of being] lactose intolerant. Because of Sergey, the child has a very, very unlikely chance of having blue eyes."[13]

Warren Buffett did a 23andMe DNA test with musician Jimmy Buffett to resolve the long-standing question of whether they were related or not. "The report came back and it said if you don't understand the results, give us a call. I did call and got Anne on the phone. She explained it again and asked if I understood it now.

I really didn't. She finally said, 'Let's put it this way. I'm more closely related to Jimmy Buffett than you are.'" [14]

Flying High

Sergey Brin's mother marvels at the height of her son's success. "It's mind-boggling," says Eugenia. "It's hard to comprehend, really. He was a very capable child in math and computers, but we could never imagine this." [15]

When asked how it felt to have sudden vast wealth, Brin said, "It takes a lot of getting used to. You always hear the phrase, money doesn't buy you happiness. But I always in the back of my mind figured a lot of money will buy you a little bit of happiness. But it's not really true. I got a new car because the old one's lease expired. Nothing terribly fancy—you could drive the same car." [16]

~

Has success and wealth changed him? "I don't think at a certain scale it matters," said Sergey, "but I do have a pretty good toy budget now. I just got a new monitor." [17]

Sergey also bought a pricey new home on the peninsula south of San Francisco and a New York apartment, but he still is careful with personal money. "From my parents I learned to be frugal and to be happy without many things." [18]

He likes to shop at Costco warehouse stores, where he bought his parents a membership. "It's a store that he knows and understands," explained Sergey's father.[19] Luckily, there is a Costco very near Google headquarters.

~

Larry Page, the intellectual of the Google guys, seeks exploration of space through his involvement in the Google Lunar X-Prize and by serving on the X-Prize board. However, Sergey, the trapeze artist, dives right in. Recently he traveled to Kazakhstan to visit the Baikonur Cosmodrome for a mini space vacation. Brin has paid $5 million to travel into actual space. He'll make the trip in 2011 with Space Adventures, a company that struck a deal with the Russian space agency to launch the first entirely private flight into space. Brin will get one of the two seats available on that mission.

LARRY PAGE

While Sergey Brin's is an immigrant's story, Larry Page, several generations away from the immigrant experience, was in most ways the typical American boy of his generation. Even so, as with Sergey, the seeds were planted early for him to pull the Prince Arthur sword from the stone of technology. Although perhaps not consciously on the part of their parents, they both were groomed from childhood for the journey they would take. Their destiny evolved from their origins.

Like his partner, Sergey Brin, Larry comes from Jewish heritage. Page's maternal grandfather immigrated to Israel, where he lived in a desert town near the Dead Sea, and worked as a tool-and-die maker. Larry's mother was raised in the Jewish faith, but his father was too scientific for much religion. His focus was on the world of technology.

Cradled in a Computer Culture

Page's grandfather was a Detroit factory worker, but his grandson has had a far different life. Lawrence Edward Page grew up in Lansing, Michigan, surrounded by math, science, and computers. His father was a highly regarded professor at Michigan State, where his mother also taught computer programming. His parents divorced when Larry was 8 years old. Nevertheless, the boy grew up with both parents in his life. Larry's funloving father took him to Grateful Dead concerts as a child.

Page explained, "my dad was a computer science professor, so we had computers really early. The first computer we owned as a family was in 1978 [Larry would have been 5 years old], the Exidy Sorcerer. It was popular in Europe but never in the U.S. It had

32K memory. My brother had to write the operating system."[20]

Larry inherited at least one of his father's traits—the tendency to have spirited discussions about everything. "In some ways [Carl] was a little hard to deal with," said George Stockman, one of Professor Page's colleagues at Michigan State, "because he wanted to argue about everything and he did, and . . . [he] shared a lot of that with his son. So intellectually they shared in a lot of discussion."[21]

Nikola Tesla, Page's Hero

Twelve-year-old Larry Page, an aspiring inventor, read a biography of Nikola Tesla, and it got him to thinking. The boy admired the phenomenal number of innovations credited to Tesla but was struck by the fact that Tesla led a life fraught with conflict, was bad with money, died in poverty, and was little-known outside scientific circles. Certainly, school children don't study Tesla the way they do Thomas Edison.

Considered the father of modern physics and electrical engineering, Tesla invented alternating current (AC) power and the AC motor. He pioneered many scientific advances including robotics, remote control, radar, and computer science. Although Marconi claimed it, Tesla was eventually recognized as the inventor of the radio. His workable inventions aside, Tesla often was regarded as a mad scientist, thanks to his behavior and a raft of wild ideas. Tesla also had difficulty commercializing or finding practical applications for his ideas and inventions and therefore did not seem to accomplish as much as he might have.

Page dreamed of being as creative and doing such great things, and he wanted his work to make a difference and change the world. Since some of Tesla's inventions did change the world, it would also seem that even at 12 years of age, Page also was aiming for recognition and financial reward.

TESLA'S STORY

In 1856, Nikola Tesla, according to legend, was born exactly at midnight during a raging electric storm, which may or may not explain his troubled life and his fascination with anything that sparked.

Tesla, a Croatian, studied in several respected Eastern European universities, but, despite his genius, never graduated. He experienced a nervous breakdown in early life but nevertheless found work in the emerging electrical power industry. When he immigrated to the United States, he went to work for Thomas Edison, but left Edison after an argument over wages. Soon, Tesla was off doing his own research and working on inventions in New York and Colorado Springs. The appeal of Colorado was the wonderful electric storms of the Rocky Mountains. Visitors to Tesla's laboratories often found him at work, surrounded by man-made lightning. Although Tesla assured them the lightning bolts were harmless, the sight terrified the visitors.

Certainly, Tesla was quirky, most likely suffering from an obsessive-compulsive disorder. He was fanatically clean, had an aversion to overweight people, and became obsessed with the number three. He often circled the block three times before entering a building, demanded three napkins at meals, and would not stay in a hotel unless the room was divisible by the number three.

Tesla may have suffered from a rare neurological condition called *synesthesia*, in which one type of stimulation evokes the sensation of another. For example, hearing a sound or thinking of a number may produce the visualization of a color.

The inventor died alone and penniless at age 86 in room 3327 of the New Yorker Hotel.

The Tesla Car

Despite his tragic story, Tesla has many admirers, one of whom named an über-chic $109,000 electric sports car after him.

The limited run of hand-built Teslas will travel up to 130 miles per hour and do 0-to-60 in about four seconds.

The Tesla also can go 250 miles on a single charge of electricity to its nearly silent motor. The car is powered by an innovative lithium-ion battery and costs a penny a mile to drive.

The car's developers chose to build a sports version because they knew the first generation of their car would be expensive, due to development costs. They also realized that many of Silicon Valley's billionaires pay homage to green technology and simple living, but also have a yen for fast cars. They have Corvettes, Porsches, and other costly sports cars tucked away in the five-car garage. They figured a whiz-bang electric model would have appeal.

During the economic crisis of 2008, Tesla Motors ran into financial trouble and has had to cut back drastically. But thanks to $40 million from an angel investor, it has been able to carry on. By the end of 2008, Tesla had orders for more than 1,200 cars, and had delivered 50 roadsters. It was shipping ten cars a week.

Both Larry and Sergey have ordered the Tesla, as have actor George Clooney and California Governor Arnold Schwarzenegger.

Motivated by Montessori

Like Sergey, Larry attended a Montessori elementary school, where he was exposed to an educational method developed by an Italian physician, Maria Montessori,[22] in the early 1920s. Her ideas quickly spread around the world. Montessori once wrote: "There is a part of a child's soul that has always been unknown but which must be known. With a spirit of sacrifice and enthusiasm we must go in search, like those who travel to foreign lands and tear up mountains in their search for hidden gold."[23]

Montessori believed that children wanted to learn and that development came in stages with each child. Playing was children's work, and by directed play, children moved along with their phases of development into deep learning. As a result, children often became more self-managing, responsible, and committed to lifelong learning. Certainly, her methods seemed to have shaped both Sergey and Larry.

"We do not want children who simply obey and are there without interest," she taught, "but we want to help them in their mental and emotional growth. Therefore, we should not try to give small ideas, but great ones, so that they not only receive them but ask for more."[24]

The Leadership Program

Later, Larry Page graduated from East Lansing High School, where he played the saxophone. He went on to graduate with honors and a degree in computer engineering from the University of Michigan. At UM, he served a term as president of Eta Kappa Nu, the National Honor Society for electrical and computer engineering students. There, and in another special program, he began developing leadership skills.

"In particular," he said, "the LeaderShape program was an amazing experience that helped me a lot when we started Google."[25] LeaderShape is a UM personal development program that originated in the early 1990s in the College of Engineering.

The Solar Racer

It also was at the University of Michigan that Larry followed his interest in alternative forms of energy. As a member of the school's solar car team, he took part in the early phase of building the champion 1993 Maize & Blue solar car.

The UM solar car ran in two races, winning a national championship in Sunrayce 93, the predecessor race to the North American Solar Challenge. It then went on to finish eleventh in the 1993 World Solar Challenge. Maize & Blue is now part of the permanent display at the Museum of Science and Industry in Chicago. The car had an evolutionary design descended from the General Motors Sunraycer and the University of Michigan's first-generation car, Sunrunner. It is considered an early demonstration of energy-efficient automobile design.

Go West, Larry

After earning his undergraduate degree, Larry headed for Stanford University. However, having spent his entire life in the familiar environment around Michigan, he set out to California with some trepidation. "At first it was pretty scary," he said. "I kept complaining to my friends that I was going to get sent home on the bus. It didn't quite happen that way, however."[26]

Tragedy struck during Larry's first year at Stanford. His father Carl, a survivor of childhood polio, died from complications of pneumonia at age 58.

"I remember Larry sitting on the steps of the Gates Building and he was very depressed," said Sean Anderson, a grad-school officemate of Larry. "A number of his friends were around trying to comfort him."[27]

Fortunately, he had family. Larry's brother Carl was living in Silicon Valley as well. Larry remains close to his mother and brother. The three of them participated in a peace march in Oregon, protesting the Iraq war.[28]

Lego-centricity

As the legend goes, Larry once built a programmable computer from Legos. Page has always had a fascination with the children's building blocks, and Google has become a Lego-centric company. Craig Silverstein recalled that the company learned a lesson about quality control early in its life, thanks to the desire to build a hard-drive case out of Legos. The original Danish version was expensive, and to save money the Google team went to a discount store and bought a knockoff of

Legos. Sadly, the quality wasn't the same. The crew came in one morning to find that their hard-drive case had crumbled into a heap sometime during the night.

Nevertheless, Larry's love of Legos continues. When asked by a reporter what his favorite technology was, he replied, "The thing I'm most fond of is Lego Mindstorms. They're little Lego kits that have a computer built in. They're like robots with sensors. I've been doing some classified things with them."[29]

Mensa Boy

As the engineer and mathematician who oversees the writing of the complex algorithms and computer programs at Google, Larry has a reputation as a deep thinker and major nerd. When he gave the keynote speech at the huge Las Vegas Consumer Electronics Show, he brought Robin Williams on stage with him. Williams mocked Page, calling him "Mensa boy." Williams piled it on, saying, "Larry, do you realize you sound just like Mister Rogers?"[30]

Larry Gets Married

"This is the wedding that everyone's been talking about in Silicon Valley," proclaimed *Valleywag* editor-in-chief Owen Thomas.[31] Larry Page wed Lucinda Southworth, his longtime girlfriend, on December 8, 2007. They were married on Necker Island, Richard Branson's Caribbean retreat. Necker Island, once a favorite spot of Princess Diana, provided appropriate privacy and security. And no wonder—rooms there start at $50,000 per week and can climb to $300,000 per week.

Southworth, a pretty blonde, achieved something Page aspired to but did not accomplish—she earned her Ph.D. Lucy studied biomedical informatics at Stanford University after graduating from the University of Pennsylvania and earning a master of science from Oxford University. Additionally, she has done medical social work in South Africa.

The X-Prize

One April Fool's Day, Google announced plans to open Googlunaplex, a research facility on the moon. It sounded like a joke, but was it? Both of the Google founders exhibit an unnatural interest in worlds beyond our own. At the *Star Trek* Fortieth Anniversary convention in Las Vegas, Google set up a booth featuring tools suitable for intergalactic use.

Yes, Googlunaplex was all in fun, but Larry and Sergey get serious about the subject of outer space. Using Google's Sky software, found within Google Earth, Web surfers can view stars and constellations and take a virtual tour of the galaxies.

Page serves on the board of directors of the X-Prize Foundation and is the corporate spirit behind the Google Lunar X-Prize, a $20 million reward to the first company to develop a successful moon-exploring robot. At least ten teams from around the globe have signed up to compete in the nongovernmental race to the moon.

The team that collects the grand prize must soft land a privately funded robotic spacecraft on the moon by December 31, 2012. The robot must be able to rove 500 meters and beam specific video, images, and data back to Earth.

Larry sees all sorts of advantages of having a permanent base on the moon, ranging from solving some of Earth's energy problems to serving as a launching pad for more distant exploration of the universe.

Ramin Khadem, chairman of one of the competitors, Odyssey Moon, explains why the competition to get a foothold on the moon—again—is so exciting. "The moon is the eighth continent and we need to exploit it in a responsible way. We want to win the Google prize and, if we do, that will be gravy. But either way we are going to the moon."[32]

The X-Prize Foundation offers several other awards for groundbreaking work that will benefit humanity with an emphasis on scientific endeavors. In addition to the space prizes, there is one for automotive advances and genomics.

No More Laundry

When asked how success and wealth had changed his life, Page replied, "I don't have to do the laundry."[33]

Laundry may be an important issue. The story goes that on the morning Google went public, Larry showed up for work, uncharacteristically, in a suit and tie. According to *GQ* magazine, he somehow sat in a plateful of crème fraiche. Sympathetic Googlers helped him remove the mess from the rear of his pants.[34]

THE POWER OF PARTNERSHIP

When Larry traveled to Stanford for an orientation visit in the spring of 1995, Sergey already was a second-year student. They met on a walking tour of the campus guided by Sergey, and as the story goes, sparks flew. Apparently, they argued about every topic they discussed, which is not surprising, considering their matching levels of self-confidence and Larry's family history of confrontational debate. Each young man considered the other somewhat arrogant and obnoxious, yet the contentious conversation also was engaging. It clearly was interesting to both of them.

Despite their verbal differences, Larry and Sergey walked on common ground. While Sergey is an extrovert and Larry is quieter, they both are playful and a little wacky. They look so much alike they could be brothers, although Sergey more resembles the character Linguini in the Pixar movie, *Ratatouille*, than Larry does. Both men are sons of college professors, they share a Jewish heritage, and both received a Montessori School education as children.

They each have one sibling, both brothers, although Sergey's brother is younger and Larry's is older. Carl Page Jr. also is a successful Silicon Valley entrepreneur. In 2000, he sold the company he founded, eGroups, to Yahoo! for $432 million.

Both Larry and Sergey are math whizzes with a towering regard for academic achievement.

Sergey admits he mostly goofed off during much of his education. "I tried so many different things in grade school," he said. "The more you stumble around the more likely you are to stumble across something valuable."[35] Sergey followed this wandering path until he met Larry. Page, it seems, didn't waste much time getting to work on his graduate project.

After Larry arrived at Stanford and conferred with his advisor, he began developing a project called "BackRub," named for its process of analyzing back links to a website. Soon Sergey was working with him on the project out of Room 360 of the William Gates Computer Science building.

They were following the tradition of their industry, the road from princes to kings—that of partnering up two amazing brains on a single project. First, there was Hewlett and Packard, and then Bill Gates and Paul Allen formed a schooldays' alliance that continued for years and changed the way the world works. Steve Jobs and Steve Wozniak followed at Apple. It happened again at Yahoo! with Jerry Yang and David Filo.

Larry and Sergey seemed to sense the nobility in their relationship, their similar brainpower, the same ideals, and the grit. With this kind of magic, all Larry and Sergey had to do was work hard and make good decisions along the way, and success was inevitable.

Okay, this sounds too easy, and in fact, few there be who can pull it off at the level Sergey and Larry were able to. It also takes imagination and an excellent idea.

Forging the Stanford Connection

Gates 360, the Stanford graduate student office shared by Larry Page and Sergey Brin, has practically become a computer science shrine. It is the birthplace of dreams, especially the dreams shared by young people excited by computers, innovation, and getting rich by launching a lollapalooza of a company.

A Creative Environment

Nearly all of the original search software and methods originated at universities. Carnegie Mellon, the University of Nevada, and the University of California at Berkeley were early development centers.

But Stanford University, inextricably linked to the scientific accomplishments of Silicon Valley and fueled by the venture capital community on nearby Sand Hill

Road, Palo Alto, has been the most fertile high-tech incubator anywhere. Hewlett-Packard, Excite, Cisco Systems, Yahoo!, and Sun Microsystems (*SUN* stands for *Stanford University Network*) and many other companies—including Google—were conceived there.

"The ecosystem we work in, our own network is really important," says venture capitalist Randy Komisar. "Where our network is strongest is right around us in Silicon Valley. It is not a surprise that a lot of companies we back coming out of Europe, Israel, even coming out of countries like India, end up with the management teams coming to Silicon Valley to build their businesses, because that ecosystem is so reinforcing to them."[36]

"We were very lucky to have been there in the early days," remember Yahoo! founders Jerry Yang and David Filo of the early 1990s. "It was virgin territory. There was so much creativity. Every time someone did some-thing novel, it was monumental."[37]

Rajeev Matwani, one of the Google advisors at the university and an angel investor in various high-stakes ventures, says, "I credit Stanford for creating an envi-ronment where people in different areas can work with each other and do things where the whole is greater than the sum of the parts."[38]

Stanford makes it easy for graduate students to pursue work that could lead to innovation and the formation of a new company. Its Office of Technology Licensing will pay for the patent process, then enter into long-term licensing agreements that let the budding scientists launch their startups, and with luck, hit the jackpot.

Stanford President John L. Hennessy says that coming out of school with a company is more productive than simply writing a thesis:

> *We have an environment at Stanford that promotes entrepreneurship and risk-taking research. You have this environment that gets people thinking about ways to solve problems that are at the cutting edge. You have an environment that is supportive of taking that out into industry. People really understand here that sometimes the biggest way to deliver an effect to the world is not by writing a paper but by taking technology you believe in and making something of it. We are an environment where a mile from campus they can talk to people who fund these companies and have lots of experience doing it.*[39]

A Poignant History

Stanford was founded in1891 to honor the memory of Leland Stanford Jr., the son of railroad magnate and California Governor Leland Stanford and his wife Jane. Leland Jr. died of typhoid just before his sixteenth birthday. Among the members of Stanford's first class was a future president, young Herbert Hoover. Stanford is at the top of its game in a number of fields of academic study, ranging from journalism to medicine.

The Stanford of today is virtually a city on its own. Its sprawling campus reflects the California landscape surrounding it, with palm, eucalyptus, and cypress groves, Mission-style architecture, and red-tiled roofs. The campus is rich with art, and students blithely pedal their bicycles among one of the best collections of Rodin sculpture anywhere. Most recent buildings seem designed to fit in, but the university's diversity of programs and its wealth have led to certain examples of more functional and less stylized architecture. Nevertheless, it is a leading-edge university, and the campus jumps with life.

Clearly, Stanford is a place where bright young people can make connections in their own field that last throughout their careers. Such has been the case for Sergey and Larry.

Because their parents taught in the field of computers and science, both young men had spent their lives in this social and political structure. They were well aware of the heady academic environment they were entering. This was where the learned sorcerers would put the crowning touch on their preparation for the future. Attending Stanford was a big deal for both of them.

An Academic or an Entrepreneur?

"I decided I was either going to be a professor or start a company. . . . I was really excited to get into Stanford. There wasn't any better place to go for that kind of aspiration. I always wanted to go to Silicon Valley."[40] At Stanford, Larry chose as his advisor the highly respected Terry Winograd, an early expert in human–computer interaction (HCI). Winograd is one of the foremost thinkers in the field of software design and is especially known for his work on natural language.

Like most computer engineers, Larry loved graphs. He viewed the Internet as perhaps the largest graph ever created, and one that was growing larger by the second. He and Winograd agreed that based on that concept, he should begin examining this link structure as a part of his graduate project. Page first called his search system "BackRub," because it seemed that he was forming search links through a back door. Between 1996 and 1998, students and faculty increasingly used the search engine, and it became apparent that the technology could be the basis for a company. (There is more about the development of the company in the sections ahead.)

A Grim Goodbye

Perhaps the most difficult consequence of building a company for both Brin and Page was the need to drop out of graduate school. Both of them dreamed of earning a Ph.D., a badge of honor in their families. At first, they took leaves of absence, and finally had to empty out their Stanford office space. In 1999, with initial funding in place (including a $25 million venture capital war chest), Brin and Page realized they would be too busy to continue their graduate studies. Winograd recalls the day, a year later, when they finally cleaned out their office: "They had this grim look on their face[s] because they had to go to Stanford with empty boxes, and leave with them full."[41]

Sergey's parents were not happy with the development, either. "We were definitely upset," said his mother. "We thought anyone in their right mind ought to get a Ph.D."[42]

NETWORKING AT ITS BEST

They left with their loaded-up cardboard boxes, but the Google guys' connection to Stanford has never ended:

• Stanford was good to Google and Google was good to Stanford. In fact, Google and Stanford are literally business partners. One of Google's main assets, the PageRank patent, is owned by Stanford University. Google paid the university in stock and cash for an exclusive licensing partnership, plus Annual royalties. The patent is exclusively licensed to Google until 2011. Typically, if the patent is producing results, it can be renegotiated at that time.

- It was one of their Stanford professors, David Cheriton, who introduced Larry and Sergey to Andy Bechtolsheim, who is not only a computer whiz, but also a wizard at spotting Silicon Valley startups, in which he invests. Cheriton became an early Google investor as well.

- Google's first employee was fellow graduate student Craig Silverstein. Silverstein now is Google's Director of Technology.

- Sergey's Ph.D. advisor, Professor Rajeev Montwani, became a company advisor when Sergey and Larry left Stanford. Montwani also was an early Google investor, holding an undisclosed amount of shares in the company.

- In 2002, Terry Winograd took a sabbatical from Stanford and became visiting researcher at Google. He spent his time there studying both the theory and practice of human-computer interaction.

- The designer of Google's logo, Ruth Kedar, was a Stanford faculty member.

- John Hennessy has served on the Google board of directors since April 2004. Before becoming president of Stanford in 2000, Hennessy held various positions, including dean of the School of Engineering and chair of the Department of Computer Science.

- Eric Schmidt has taught business courses, part time, at Stanford.

- For both Larry and Sergey, the Stanford connection became personal when they married women they met there. Sergey wed the daughter of the head of the physics department, Anne Wojcicki.
- Larry Page married Stanford graduate Lucy Southworth.

BURNING MAN

Just days after Google went public, the founders headed out to Burning Man, an indication, say friends, that wealth hadn't changed their priorities.

One of the first Google doodles was a stick figure added to the standard logo. It signaled to employees that Larry and Sergey had slipped away to make the long drive into Nevada's Black Rock Desert for the notorious festival of personal freedom.

They and Eric Schmidt are among the nearly 50,000 people who gather for the event each Labor Day week in one of the most barren and desolate landscapes anywhere. In fact, Larry and Sergey took a special interest in Schmidt when they interviewed him for the potential CEO of Google because he was the only candidate who attended Burning Man. Friends say that Larry and Sergey have received lots of inspiration from Burning Man.

Burning Man—from its 1986 start on San Francisco's Baker Beach through its evolution into the bustling city it has become—always has been strange. It's art, it's music, it's lifestyle, it's freewheeling behavior and attire (or lack of attire)—it's an outpost for radical personal expression. The ritual torching of a 40-foot effigy of a man has become almost secondary to all the other activities.

Those who show up must provide entirely for their own needs, and they come expecting (and no doubt hoping for) anything: A federal government employee was astounded to run into her boss strolling through Black Rock City (BRC). He was dressed in boots, chaps, a cowboy hat, and nothing else. A photograph circulates on the Internet of Schmidt at Burning Man, dressed modestly in a cotton-candy-pink cowboy shirt and hat. He was wearing pants.

If you go looking for Larry, Sergey, or even Eric at the gathering of the tribe, don't expect to spot them. They surely will be tricked out in elaborate costumes and face makeup.

Adult
Supervision

Eric Schmidt is sometimes called "the third leg of Google." Like the third leg on a stool, he helps keep balance. And even though his background is in technology, he also moves the Google business model forward in a decisive, purposeful way.

Although they had promised their venture capitalists that they would hire a seasoned CEO for Google, Larry and Sergey were at first slow to do so. The two couldn't find anyone who suited their style. Venture capitalists John Doerr and Michael Mortiz were pushing them to get on with it. They finally sent the Google guys someone they had seen in action before: Dr. Eric Schmidt. All of this happened three years before Google became a public company.

Schmidt now shares responsibility for Google's daily operations with Larry and Sergey, and as CEO he has legal responsibility for the company's vice presidents and the sales organization.

Schmidt has been described as more of a pragmatist than a visionary, a low-keyed leader and a skilled collaborator.

After Schmidt had been at Google for a while, he and Brin and Page made an informal pact to stay together in the Google venture for at least 20 years.

"We agreed the month before we went public that we should work together for twenty years," said Schmidt. By the time the agreement is fulfilled, Schmidt will be 69 years old; Page will be 51, and Brin 50.[1]

Known for his slogan, "Don't fight the Internet,"[2] Schmidt is credited with positioning Google smack in the middle of nearly every important development related to the commercialization of the Web.

THE COLLECTIVE WISDOM OF SILICON VALLEY

Eric Emerson Schmidt was born in the spring of 1955 in Washington, D.C. After graduating from high school in Yorktown, Virginia, he earned an electrical engineering degree from Princeton University and then a doctorate in computer science from the University of California at Berkeley.

Schmidt earned his tech stripes toiling in the ranks of respected Silicon Valley veteran organizations. He worked at a series of companies, including Bell Labs, Zilog, and Xerox's legendary Palo Alto Research Center (PARC). He progressed to chief technology officer at Sun Microsystems, and then to chief executive officer of Novell. When Novell was acquired by Cambridge Technology Partners, Schmidt left the company, making him available for recruitment by Google.

Though the implication that Schmidt provides adult supervision to impetuous young men may rankle, occasionally Schmidt's parental proclivity has popped up in public. At one meeting, Larry Page was asked about his opinion of the U.S. PATRIOT Act, legislation that some people fear impinges on personal privacy. Larry started to reply with theoretical comments about the Act, when Schmidt interrupted, "The best way to answer that is, it's the law of [the] land and we have to follow it."[3]

(For more about privacy, see the section "Privacy Issue" in the chapter "Google Grows Up.")

HE'S BEEN THE ROCK; THEY'VE BEEN THE ROCKETS

Schmidt's well-seasoned perspective has been an effective complement to the Google founders' youthful exuberance and impatient goals. Schmidt seems to telegraph reliability and stability. Yet, despite his down-to-earth demeanor, Schmidt encourages people to "set audacious goals."[4] To their credit, Larry and Sergey had enough acumen to choose Schmidt as a partner, and clearly they have learned from him.

At Google's 2008 annual meeting, Schmidt declared that the Google guys had grown up:

> *They now function in the company as the senior executives with the kind of skills and experience. . . .*

At that point Larry interrupted, ". . . we wish we had five years ago."

Schmidt continued:

> *Now we don't have the same kind of arguments. In fact, they really are running the companies that they founded at the scale and with the insights that you would expect of people who are no longer young founders but are mature business leaders.*[5]

A MAN OF INFLUENCE

Thanks to Google stock options, Schmidt ranks as the 126th richest person in the world, according to *Forbes*. Schmidt also serves on Princeton University's and Apple's board of directors.

As for his personal life, Schmidt and his wife, Wendy, live in Atherton, California. They collect modern art and the work of contemporary artists and run a family foundation that makes contributions to environmental and economic sustainability projects. He is an avid private pilot, which may explain Google's interesting fleet of aircraft.

Toward the end of the 2008 presidential campaign, Schmidt came out in favor of Barack Obama and began stumping the campaign trail with the candidate. Despite Schmidt's preference, most of the 2008 presidential candidates, including Hillary Clinton and John McCain, visited Googleplex and spoke with employees.

Schmidt explained his personal position this way:

Well, people give for all—for all sorts of reasons, but my own view is that Senator Obama, now president-elect Obama, touched a chord when he talked about making the world a better place for all of us. His focus on the middle class, his focus on making education stronger, his focus on science, and his focus on doubling the research budget. All things which have largely been ignored under the current administration, those are the things that I think that really hit a chord and of course they didn't hit a chord with the opposition.[6]

Obama told voters that Schmidt would be among the business leaders to be advising him if he were elected president. Schmidt's name was at the top of the list to be named Obama's cabinet-level technology advisor, but

Schmidt said he wasn't interested in the post. After the 2008 election, Schmidt appeared on CNBC's *Mad Money*, and Jim Cramer asked him about the possibility:

> *CRAMER: All right, but look, here's what I would do if I were (Obama). I would say, okay, Eric, you talk a good game. I want you to resign from Google and come to work for me as my chief tech czar. If called, would you do it?*

> *SCHMIDT: I love working at Google, and I'm happy at Google, so the answer is no.*[7]

Perhaps Schmidt also demurred due to his commitment to stay with Google for the long haul.

Because of his work with President Obama and labors on behalf of the quest for viable alternative energy sources, Schmidt has been in the public eye. Nancy Litwack-Strong, a *Denver Post* reader, who grew up in a home where *mensch* was a word of high praise, responded to a column about Schmidt this way:

> *After reading Al Lewis' column on Sunday, I feel compelled to call Google CEO Eric Schmidt a mensch. He understands the societal functions that our taxes support, he appreciates the opportunities to succeed that he has had in this country, and he is happy to do his fair share to keep our country great and keep our country strong. I wish more people thought like him.*[8]

Despite this impression, some say Schmidt can be quite harsh. Rumors circulate on the Internet about his personal life and some consider him a Svengali, just as interested in controlling the world as changing it. Certainly, he has taken a hard line on copyright and privacy issues. While he claims to align with the interests of Internet searchers, he clearly aligns with Google's best chances to sell advertising.

CLIMBING A DIFFERENT KIND OF MOUNTAIN

Is there anything in his life Schmidt wants to accomplish and hasn't yet done? Yes, there is. "I've always wanted to climb Mt. Everest," he told a gathering of NASA scientists. "When you look at me, clearly that's not going to happen."[9] He has, though, climbed vicariously using Google Earth, and he found Everest to be extremely cold.

In the
Beginning

From the time they met in 1996 until 1998, Larry and
Sergey continued to experiment with various search
ideas. Larry began studying the importance of links
with his own homepage on the Stanford website. With
the search engine he named BackRub, he wrote and
improved on search code based on links between
websites.

Page and Brin soon latched onto two big ideas. The
first was based on BackRub but was renamed "Page-
Rank" after Larry Page. PageRank treated the number of
times a site was linked to others as a rough measure
of its authority. The second was to automate and sanctify
the search process and to cope with the ever-increasing
number of sites. In order to give some objectivity to
the results, humans could work with the algorithm,

but never tinker with the search results. (This still is mostly true. However, with the introduction of Google's SearchWiki, searchers themselves can tailor the results in various ways.)

Once Larry and Sergey had defined the new way to search and deliver the results, they were faced with two more major problems: how to collect the entire World Wide Web into one database and how to find enough computer power to store and process the huge volumes of information.

The pair scrounged around to collect computers for the project, often haunting the Stanford loading docks for machinery to borrow. The first version of Google was released in August 1996, on the Stanford Web. The address was google.stanford.edu.

Very quickly Stanford grew weary of the burden the two grad students were placing on its system. They in turn outgrew Stanford's capacity to provide equipment and to handle the burgeoning number of search requests coming in. A little over a year later, Sergey and Larry took the search engine off Stanford servers because Google took up too much bandwidth. In 1997, Google.com was registered as a domain name.

The need for physical equipment continued to explode. Without initial resources, Larry and Sergey found computers and equipment wherever they could. They cobbled together inexpensive PCs to hold their data. They got a good deal on a terabyte of disks and built their own computer housings in Larry's dorm room. The dorm room became their first data center. "Larry would scour the world to save a penny," recalled Charles Orgish, Stanford's head of computer systems.[1]

What started as a necessity soon became one of Google's competitive advantages. They found that their jerry-rigged computer system was easy to repair and modify. "Others assumed large servers were the fastest way to handle massive amounts of data. Google found networked PCs to be faster," explained Google on its Corporation Information Web page.

Venture capitalist and Google board member John Doerr says that Google uses "pile-up" computing. It piles up a bunch of computers, connects them, and builds a data center. The way the machines are set up, when one breaks down the entire system does not break down. The crippled machine is ignored and the work of processing queries continues.

By mid-1998, Sergey set up a business office, and the pair began contacting potential partners who might want to license a superior search engine.

They hoped to sell Google through the venture capital firm of Kleiner Perkins Caulfield & Byers. They shopped the company around at $1 million. Alta Vista, Excite, and the now-defunct Infoseek were among the companies that saw no commercial benefit to Google.

No doubt to their everlasting regret, these companies passed. Larry and Sergey had no luck finding a buyer.

The young entrepreneurs faced a daunting problem. While they were passionate about their project, at that time few others in the computer industry saw Internet search as an important aspect of their work.

However, when Larry and Sergey called on David Filo, one of the founders of Yahoo!, he recognized the value of their technology but encouraged them to go forward with forming their own company the way he and Jerry Yang had done. "When it's fully developed and scalable," Filo said, "let's talk again."[2]

It wasn't the answer they were hoping for, but it gave them encouragement. And Filo did point them in the right direction. The disappointment in not being able to sell their work may have been the greatest stroke of luck in their lives so far.

"That people were concentrating on other things was crucial," recalls Craig Silverstein, the college friend who was the first to join Page and Brin as an employee. "It's very possible that if someone had been truly interested in our technology, we would have just sold to them."

"We recognized that a lot of companies don't make it," added Silverstein, now Google's director of technology. "The venture capitalists tried to scare us, saying that 80 percent of start-ups fail. Larry shot back with: 'Yes, but most of those are restaurants.'"[3]

Going it alone was a risk, but Larry's self-confidence showed up early in the Google game. His advisor, Terry Winograd, felt the students had a viable product but knew they needed to move off campus and begin acting like a real company. That took money that Sergey and Larry didn't yet have. "I don't see how you're ever going to get the money," lamented Winograd. Larry replied, "Well, you're going to see. We'll figure that out."[4]

Ruth Kedar, who designed the Google logo, said she felt the Google guys came to her with vision, direction, and optimism. "In general," said Kedar, "when people speak about their big dreams in life, they apologize many times for it, for the pretension. They (Brin and Page) weren't like that. It was clear to them from the start that they had something big on their hands."[5]

Google's corporate page noted that despite the quivery beginning, Google was on its way by the late 1990s. "Clearly we evolved," says the Google website. "What had been a college research project was now a real company offering a service that was in great demand. So on September 21, 1999, the beta label came off Google.com."

THE ULTIMATE SEARCH ENGINE

In 1996, Larry came up with the notion of using links between Web pages to rank their relative importance to searchers. The more links a website had, the more likely it was to contain the most useful information. The concept sounds simple; executing the idea was a little more complicated. Nevertheless, it didn't take long for Page's brainchild to dominate the world of Internet search.

People use Google more than 200 million times a day in more than 100 languages, from Kurdish to Klingon, and it does deliver the results in a flash. Google searches five billion Web pages for links in two-tenths of a second.

By early November 2008, Google's share of domestic Web searches grew to 71.7 percent, compared with 17.7 percent by its closest competitor, Yahoo!, and 5.4 percent by third-ranking Microsoft. Google also ruled the search business financially, claiming 76 percent of the 2008 market in terms of revenue.[6]

One of the reasons for Google's success is that people like the results. But adding to that, Google is ubiquitous. It is constantly before the eyes of most people using the Internet. Google has been able to provide search services for a large number of Internet operations, including America OnLine (AOL) and the free Web browser, Mozilla Firefox. In 2007, the Mozilla Foundation received $66 million, or 88 percent of its $75 million in revenues, from a partnership with Google.

Yet Larry and Sergey believe that Google still is in the early stages of development. The search engine of the future will be so much more intuitive, more along the lines of a superintelligence—a reference librarian who knows everything there is to know and how to find it.

Google's Marissa Mayer wonders why search has to be with words. "Why can't I enter my query as a picture of the birds overhead and have the search engine identify what kind of bird it is? Why can't I capture a snippet of audio and have the search engine identify and analyze it (a song or stream of conversation) and tell me any relevant information about it?"

"If anybody thinks the future of search is going to look like the present search, that's crazy," said Microsoft CEO Steve Ballmer. "The user interface on search hasn't changed for six years. You still get the same dull, boring 10 blue links, for God's sake. Can't we do better than that?"[8]

NOT INVENTING, BUT IMPROVING UPON

Internet search was going on long before the Google boys attacked the problem of achieving meaningful results from searches. Although they didn't invent the concept of search, they vastly improved upon search techniques.

Susan Wojcicki, whose home served as Google's incubator, recalls many early discussions about search. "Not another but a better search engine," she said. "From the beginning they had a very clear vision that they could build something much better than what existed at the time."[9]

Google's Corporate Information Web page explains, "Where others accepted apparent speed limits imposed by search algorithms, Google wrote new algorithms that proved there were no limits. And Google continues to work on making it all go even faster."

Long before Google came along, newspapers, magazines, and newly established websites believed it was possible to reap rewards from Internet advertising. None were very good at it. Yet today, Google dominates that business. Google perfected an advertising concept developed by a company called GoTo.com, which later was renamed Overture and sold to Yahoo!. From e-mail to cell phone platforms, Google has a history of coming in late and making it better.

There are multiple examples of how Google either borrowed or bought concepts and made them better and more usable:

- The company acquired its hypnotic satellite-imagery application when it acquired Keyhole, the firm that developed the technology.
- In 2005, Google bought the popular photo-sharing site, Flickr.
- There were many map services before Google launched Google Earth, but none of them achieved the same popular appeal.

While Google is best known for building on existing technology, the company has patented around 113 new ideas in its first ten years of existence. For more on how Google does it, check out the section "20 Percent Projects" in the chapter "Google Culture."

LOOK AROUND YOU FOR INSPIRATION

Larry Page says that he finds tremendous inspiration in the science already out there. He demonstrated to a group of students the way a small, mouse-like robot was able to scurry over obstacles quickly and easily as it went about its work. "This is a pretty cool thing. I've never seen anything quite like this before. And it turns out that it's ten times cheaper than all other robots like it," said Page.

What makes the robot different and more effective than others is that it doesn't use intelligence to move forward and find its way; instead it has springs for legs. It just bounds along the way cockroaches do. If it hits an obstacle, it springs in a different direction. Someone has already invented the springing robot, but the idea behind it can be applied elsewhere.

"This has great implications if you're building robots, for example," Page noted. "If you find one of these [ideas] and use it as a foundation for a company or an invention or entrepreneurship you're in a much stronger business position and that's a great place to be if you're starting a company."[10]

HOW SEARCH WORKS

Google rocks. It raises my perceived IQ by at least 20 points.
I can pull a reference or quote in seconds, and I can figure out
who I'm talking to and what they're known for—a key feature
for those of us who are name-memory challenged.

—*Wes Boyd, president, MoveOn.org*[11]

Google once claimed that pigeons powered its search results, but that was just another April Fool's Day joke.

It is estimated that in 2007 Google was processing more than 37 billion searches per month, compared with 8.5 billion by Yahoo! and 2.2 billion by Microsoft. Most people search out information on the Internet, often multiple times each day. Yet few people comprehend how search really works.

In simplified form, it goes something like this:

Step #1: You enter a word or series of words, and the search engine connects you to those words in a database it has created. From the outset, Larry and Sergey aimed at putting the entire Internet into its database. The company still strives to do that, plus adding many other sources of information.

Step #2: The engine searches, using three major segments:

1. The *crawl*, which actually doesn't crawl. Rather, it broadcasts requests to thousands of Web pages seeking your search words. The crawler also is called a *spider*.
2. The *index*, a massive database where the words are stored and found.
3. The *runtime system*—also called a *query processor*. This step delivers search results back to the questioner.

This scenario, however, doesn't explain exactly how Google's unique search works. That code is a company trade secret. But Larry Page, who came up with the original idea, gives us some clues.

Soon after arriving at Stanford, Page began meeting with his doctoral program advisor, Terry Winograd, to discuss projects. "We settled on looking at the link structure on the Web," said Page, "how to grab all the links and analyze them and do something interesting. We eventually wound up with a way to rank Web pages based on the link, then realized we could build a better search engine. And we did just that."[12]

The Google website expands on Page's explanation:

Instead of relying on a group of editors or solely on the frequency with which certain terms appear, Google

> *ranks every web page using a breakthrough technique
> called PageRank. PageRank evaluates all of the sites
> linking to a web page and assigns them a value, based
> in part on the sites linking to them. By analyzing the full
> structure of the web, Google is able to determine which
> sites have been "voted" the best sources of information
> by those most interested in the information they offer.*[13]

Larry named PageRank, the program that elevated
Google over other search methods, after himself. He
started with a concept that he was familiar with, one
used in academic research. That is, a publication's
importance is determined by the number of citations it
receives in other significant journals. Peer review determines a publication's relevance and reliability.

Again, Google's Technology page explains how the
process gets more complicated:

> *PageRank relies on the uniquely democratic nature of
> the web by using its vast link structure as an indicator
> of an individual page's value. In essence, Google inter-
> prets a link from page A to page B as a vote, by page A,
> for page B. But Google looks at considerably more
> than the sheer volume of votes, or links the page
> receives. For example, it also analyzes the page that
> casts the vote. Votes cast by pages that are themselves
> "important" weigh more heavily and help to make
> other pages "important." Using these and other factors,*

Google provides its views on the pages' relative importance.[14]

And that's still only part of the protocol. It's almost impossible to fathom, but PageRank considers more than 500 variables and 3 billion terms and still manages to deliver results in fractions of a second. Yet there also is a certain simplicity to the search process.

"By the way," observed Stanford Professor Rajeev Motwani, an early Google investor, "you might have noticed that the job of the search engine is nothing more than what a humble librarian does all the time and more intelligently! However, the automation in the software comes to our rescue in coping with the exponential rise in information."[15]

PLATFORM POWER

When people in the computer/Internet world use the word *platform*, it has multiple levels of meaning. At times they appear to be talking about hardware. Other times, it's software, and then it can be the Internet itself or a particular website or search engine. It can in fact refer to any one of these elements.

"Platforms are the playing field," explains John McDougall, a Chicago-based computer expert:

Big platforms are generally industry-wide and with an agreed upon set of standards which are developed and controlled by a standards group. In the case of the Internet, that group is the World Wide Web Consortium. Smaller platforms are also playing fields, but more specific in their range or scope. Who controls the standards or rules for these? The playing field determines who can use or who can play with the platform.[16]

A platform represents an infrastructure of some kind. It is a framework on which to build an economy, a society, or a corporation. So, in the world of technology, a platform is an operating system, together with the hardware on which it runs.

Google, YouTube, Facebook, Flickr, and similar platforms have four main powers that constitute genuine and valuable authority:

1. The power to set the rules of behavior
2. The power to preserve and exploit user-generated content
3. The power to promote and feature preferred content
4. The power to define the types of interaction available to users

Professor Joel West, who teaches in the computer program at San Jose State, says all of this is true, but those who operate platforms need people who provide third-party products and services, an ecosystem that helps the platform operate. Often this ecosystem includes companies that are competitive in some area. Google's Android software, for example, competes with Apple's iPhone, but they cooperate on other projects when both can profit from that. Experts in the field have dubbed this survival tool *coopetition*.

Google is thought to have the most powerful and extensive computing network—both in its physical equipment and in its database—in existence.

"If you printed out the index, it would be 70 miles high right now. We have all this computation," said Page. "We have about 6,000 computers, so we have a lot of resources available. We have enough space to store like 100 copies of the whole Web. So you have a really interesting sort of confluence of a lot of different things: a lot of computation, a lot of data that didn't used to be available."[17]

Google is striving to maximize its platform power in every way it can. This is one of the reasons the company has branched into mobile-phone technology. The personal computer has been the dominant platform for accessing the Internet around the world. However, in many places, Internet access by mobile phone is outpacing wireless access from a computer. There is an extensive base of mobile phones globally, and wireless networks are expanding daily.

OPEN PLATFORM

While Google waves the flag for open platforms, the details of their own platforms often are carefully guarded secrets.

At a 2008 Web 2.0 conference, Google's vice president of engineering, Vic Gundotra, argued that control of the platform by a single provider by definition slows down innovation. This was a veiled reference to Gundotra's former employer, Microsoft. Microsoft executive David Treadwell was on the same panel. He challenged Google to release into the community the driving technology of its business, its search engine, and ad platforms. Gundotra shot back that he wasn't advocating total control, and that a balance could be struck between business interests and the broader interests of the community.[18]

San Jose State's Joel West says that the term *open* has disintegrated into a marketing term, and Google is disingenuous when it implies it is an open platform. "Every platform is open to some degree and closed to some degree. This is necessary if the company is to continue as a business. Google may be more open than most companies." But West says that few of its products are fully open. "Android is not open. To say so is misleading. Only a small number of (chosen) people have access to its code." Google Books, he says, is closed, because no other Internet provider can use the books. Even readers have limited access, which is controlled entirely by Google.[19]

Google By Any Other Name

Part of Google's instant attraction is its quirky name. It's fun to say "Google it." It's easy to remember. It has a ring to it. Somehow, it isn't as entertaining to say "Yahoo! it" or "MSN it," or even "Go to it." *Google* is one of those words that is inherently amusing, and in fact, many years ago there was a cartoon character named Barney Google. The comic strip inspired the zany 1923 song, "Barney Google, with the Goo-Goo-Googly Eyes."

A BLESSED BLUNDER

It was Larry and Sergey's idea to name the company *googol*—the mathematical term for the number 1 followed by 100 zeros. Milton Sirotta, a nephew of the great mathematician Edward Kasner, coined the word. It was popularized in a book Kasner co-authored, *Mathematics and the Imagination*. The founders felt that the name *googol* would reflect Google's ambitious goal of organizing and making available all of the world's information.

Fortunately, someone misspelled *googol*, and the bungled version, *Google*, took hold. It was just as well. As it turns out, the term *googol* wasn't available for a website name, anyway.

FROM NOUN TO VERB

Google's founders were worried from the outset that they would lose control of their company name. In the prospectus they wrote that "there is a risk that the word 'Google' could become so commonly used that it becomes synonymous with the word 'search.' If this happens, we could lose protection for this trademark, which could result in other people using the word 'Google' to refer to their own products, thus diminishing our brand."

It did happen. Oddly, the first recorded use of Google as a verb was in an early e-mail that Larry Page sent to friends and fellow students. He told them to "Keep Googling." With breathtaking speed, the noun *Google* became a verb as everyone went to their computers to Google everyone else, or even to Google themselves.

Google the verb was added to the *Oxford English Dictionary* in 2006, but it wasn't cause for celebration at the company. As expected, executives at Google growled over the possibility of brand dilution and other dark implications.

PLAYING WITH THE NAME

One Web jokester surmised that *Google* is just a clever play on words—and the name really means "Go ogle." It could very well work that way. People love to play with the name. The search engine name spawned a whole list of derivative words.

As Google, Microsoft, and Yahoo! locked horns in a convoluted business deal, Internet wags talked about a possible new company, Microhoogle.

Recent headlines in the United Kingdom declared that the country suffered from *discomgooglation*, a term describing how frustrated people felt when they couldn't access the Internet. Then there is:

Googly—used within the company to describe anything that is compatible with Google culture

Googleplex—company headquarters in Mountain View, California

Googlers—those who work at Google

Googlian—anything derived from a Google concept

Googlicious—just peachy—wonderful in the Google way

And no doubt there are oodles of Googles to come.

THE GOOGLE LOGO

Google's public image is further enhanced by the delightfully simple crayon-colored logo and its placement on its spare home page. The logo makes Google seem approachable and friendly.

Reminiscent of the letters on children's building blocks, it quickly evolved into one of the world's most recognizable corporate insignias. Google's logo recognition is right up there with Nike's swoosh, NBC's peacock, and Coca Cola's red-and-white scripted name.

Brin and Page were toying with logo ideas, struggling to come up with a symbol that expressed the emerging Google culture. They asked Ruth Kedar, a graphic designer and assistant professor at Stanford, to produce some prototypes. "I had no idea at the time that Google would become as ubiquitous as it is today, or that their success would be of such magnitude," Kedar says.[1]

Kedar, who was born in Brazil but grew up and was educated in Israel, was impressed that the young men with a chancy startup insisted on paying for the logo. She only wishes she had taken payment in Google shares.

The logo as we know it today gives the impression that it was a quick-and-easy sketch-up, whereas in fact it went through many changes in the design process. Kedar began with a first try that Sergey had created with free design software.

"Someone who sees the logo for the first time doesn't necessarily need to absorb all the layers and considerations behind every decision," said Kedar. "It's better for him to discover something new every time."[2]

Kedar says the logo, both the letters and colors, is intended to convey the message that Internet search with Google will be simple, strong, and fun. She's not concerned about the frequent comment that any child could have created the Google logo. The comment, she believes, speaks to the effectiveness of the design. "It somewhat amuses me to turn on the computer and look at the logo I designed," said Kedar. "But it also fills me with pride. When you say Google to people today, they immediately see the colorful logo."[3]

She added that the *Google doodle*, the enhancements drawn by Dennis Hwang, don't bother her one bit. They play with the logo in a "very nice way."

THE GOOGLE DOODLE

A 2008 survey indicated that more than 75 percent of Britons said they couldn't live without the Internet, and 50 percent claimed that the Internet was more important than religion.[4] The Queen of England herself has become a computer user and Internet surfer, so it was natural that she would want to visit the Google office not far from Buckingham Palace. On the morning of her visit, Google users in the United Kingdom logged onto a special logo, one displaying the Queen's cheery face.

It was in the UK that Google held its first nationwide Doodle 4 Google contest, using the theme "My Britain." The winner was 13-year-old Katherine Chisnall of Trowbridge, whose doodle was displayed on the national Google website, but not on the same day Queen Elizabeth II was so honored. Chisnall's design displayed the Union Jack colors and five wonders of Britain, including Shakespeare and a castle. She won a trip to California to visit Googleplex and work with Hwang.

It has become a tradition to tweak the logo for special occasions. Susan Wojcicki first came up with the idea of "doodles," or playing with the emblem for holidays or notable events. Her original doodle was an alien landing on Google. Now Hwang provides Valentine logos, Christmas logos, and spontaneous surprise logos. For one Halloween, it was a dark-and-stormy Google, with a leering jack-o-lantern for one of the Os and a dripping candle for the L. During the 2008 Olympics, the second O in Google was replaced by a series of cartoon athletes, including a runner, a bicyclist, and a diver. The Olympic diver was appropriate, since Sergey Brin has dabbled in high diving.

GOOGLE ZEITGEIST

Writers of the past had absinthe, whiskey, or heroin. I have Google. I go there intending to stay five minutes and next thing I know, seven hours have passed, I've written 43 words, and all I have to show for it is that I know the titles of every episode of *Nanny and the Professor.*

—Michael Chabon, author,
The Amazing Adventures of Kavalier & Clay

One day when the cartoon character Drabble congratulated his boss for being the first human being ever to fail the Turing test, "Turing test" became the most searched word on Google. This was a testament to the popularity of Drabble and a clue to the Zeitgeist of newspaper readers.

So here we are at one of the most entertaining and even useful unintended consequences of a great search engine—Zeitgeist. Google makes it possible to gauge what a great many people are thinking about and possibly considering doing at any one time. The sense of anonymity of the Internet engenders an astounding level of frankness.

The word *Zeitgeist* comes from the German language, but traces its roots to Latin. It is a translation of *genius seculi. Genius* is the Latin word for "guardian spirit," and *seculi* means "of the century." The word has come to describe the intellectual and cultural climate of an era.

In the past, writers such as F. Scott Fitzgerald and artists like Salvador Dali have captured Zeitgeist, but never before has there been such an accurate, to-the-moment scientific measure as the one created by Google.

Google Zeitgeist, in several forms, tracks all the searches done on the website and ranks them by frequency of search. Hot Trends, introduced in 2007, lists the 100 most active queries at any moment. There is a monthly list and a *grande* annual list.

At times, our Zeitgeist seems shallow, with searchers tracking celebrities, celebrity rumors, and questions such as "Who is Buckethead?" There are indications that the majority of searchers are young, since names like singer Britney Spears and *High School Musical* star Vanessa Hudgens figure prominently.

Even so, some practical searchers ask how to crochet, how to flirt, or when daylight saving time begins. Enigmatically, "how to levitate" shows up, too.

In 2008, Republican vice presidential candidate and Alaska Governor Sarah Palin headed the Zeitgeist list worldwide. Next ranked was the Beijing Olympics, with the presidential candidate Barack Obama coming in sixth.

Despite the flimsy and transitory nature of search queries, author John Battelle calls Zeitgeist the database of intentions, a remarkable anthropological device of our times. Google's own website declares, "What you see here is a cumulative snapshot of interesting queries people are asking, over time, within country domains and some on Google.com—that perhaps reveals a bit of the human condition." Anyone can log on to Google.com and check on what's up almost anywhere.

One lesson from observing Zeitgeist is that Google does not set taste; rather it measures it. It tells us the silly, sad, and sometimes shocking truth about ourselves and what we actually do on the Internet as it responds to our queries and translates that into relevant search results.

~

Google regularly holds invitation-only Google Zeitgeist Conferences around the world so that thought leaders can discuss and ponder the spirit of the times. David Cameron, controversial head of the British Conservative Party, was keynote speaker at both the 2006 conference in Europe and the 2007 conference in San Francisco. Cameron described the Internet revolution, and Google's role, as the next stage of societal development, beginning with feudalism, and then from centralized state bureaucracy to one of enormous individual influence and control. Cameron welcomed the struggle between industry leaders and governments to define and direct the revolution, quoting Edmund Burke from

200 years ago: "The reciprocal struggle of discordant powers will draw out the harmony of the universe."[5]

Despite Google's revelations, there remains something mysterious and magical about Zeitgeist. Even the most creative people don't know where it comes from. George Bernard Shaw once said, "What I say today everybody will say tomorrow, though they will not remember who put it into their heads. Indeed they will be right for I never remember who puts things into my head, it is the Zeitgeist."

(*Note:* Buckethead is a mutant guitar virtuoso, American Brian Carroll, who wears a white bucket on his head while playing music.)

A Company Is Born

Sergey says that luck played a big part in the early success of the company: "We became profitable just as the market (for Internet stocks) tanked. If we had started six months later, it might have been a different story."[1]

Rajeev Motwani, the Stanford professor who advised graduate students Larry and Sergey, remembers how it all happened. The World Wide Web, he said, was coming into its own:

Sergey Brin and Larry Page were running a search engine out of Stanford. These 21-year-olds would come in and make demands on me—we need more disk space because we're crawling the Web and it's getting bigger, we need to buy more disks. . . . I'd give them more money and they'd go buy more disks. At some

point these guys said, we want to do a company.
Everybody said, you must be out of your minds. There
are like 37 search engines out there and what are you
guys going to do? How are you going to raise money,
how will you build a company and these two guys
said, we'll just do it and they went off and did it.

The next thing Motwani knew, the pair had built a global enterprise. "It's just amazing, just feels like a part of
a little bit of history and I contributed a little bit to that
history. Now I have become a start-up junkie."[2]

At first, they tried and failed to sell their technology.
At that point, Page and Brin gave up and returned to
their research. They knew there was still life in the idea
and followed David Filo's advice to begin their own
company.

YAHOO! DREW THE MAP

The parallels between Yahoo! and Google are almost
spooky. Two bored Ph.D. candidates at Stanford, looking
for a way to win a fantasy basketball league, came up
with the idea for Yahoo!. Jerry Yang and David Filo won
the sports pool, and not long afterward realized they
had created something with economic potential. They
took a whimsical and fun approach to business, and in
naming their company they started with the Internet
jargon for "yet another," *YA*. They came up with the rest

of it: *Yet Another Hierarchical Officious Oracle*. Yahoo! was born.

- Yahoo!'s main goal was to help their Stanford buddies locate intriguing websites.
- The system uses "content-based" search.
- Yahoo! earns its money from advertising.
- After a while, the 20-something entrepreneurs hired a "grown-up" businessman, Tim Koogle, to help run and develop the business. Naturally, he was a Stanford graduate.
- The company went through a stage of hypergrowth and success, launching an IPO with a multibillion-dollar market capitalization.

"We were unique," said Yang. "We were the first in this business to build a credible, sustainable, and likeable brand. If you believe the Internet is the next big medium, and if you realize every medium has had a brand associated with it like CNN with cable, then it's conceivable that Yahoo! will become one of those brands".[3]

Yahoo! was formed about five years before Google came along, and in many ways, the relationship between the two companies goes way back and was close. Google pitched Yahoo! on buying the search engine, but were sent away with nothing more than sound counsel. Yahoo! soon chose Google as its default search engine, and a day later, Yahoo! purchased eGroups for $413 million, a company that Larry's brother, Carl Page, helped to found. For a while, starting in June 2000, Google's and Yahoo!'s paths were linked. Providing search results for Yahoo! and other websites got Google off to a strong start. Before long, Google began to look like a competitor, and eventually Yahoo! dropped Google and developed its own search technology.

Sadly, after a terrifically successful run, Yahoo! fell victim to a horrendous business blunder. Microsoft made a big offer for the company but dropped it when it considered Yahoo!'s counteroffer too high. The Google founders wanted to help Yahoo! remain independent and struck an advertising arrangement. However, Google's help turned out to be no help at all. Read more about that in the section entitled "Google, Microsoft, and the Internet Civil War," in the chapter "The Dominant Power in the Industry?"

THE REQUISITE GARAGE

The story of a high-tech company starting in a California garage is a cliché for sure. Perhaps it is a required step on the path to success. As far back as 1938, Stanford graduates Bill Hewlett and Dave Packard began their company in a Palo Alto garage. Steve Jobs and Steve Wozniak built their first Apple computer in a garage in the nearby community of Los Altos.

When Google had to move out of Gates 360, their Stanford graduate school office, and Larry's Stanford dorm room, Page and Brin rented a spare bedroom and garage space in the home of Sergey's girlfriend's sister, Susan Wojcicki. Wojcicki insisted that they enter the house through the garage.

"It's a very humble house, less than 2,000 square feet," Wojcicki said of 232 Santa Margarita Avenue.[4] Wojcicki bought the Menlo Park residence shortly after earning her MBA in 1998. The purchase price was about $600,000. She rented part of it to help cover the mortgage. The four-bedroom ranch-style house on a tree-lined street proved convenient for the young entrepreneurs, since it came with a washer, dryer, hot tub, and parking spaces.

Just eight years after its beginning on Santa Margarita Avenue, Google purchased the now-historic property. Google did not reveal the price it paid, but the value of the truly modest house by 2006 was estimated at $1.2 million.

A nice profit on real estate isn't all that Susan Wojcicki got from being the landlady. She took an early job at the company and now is one of Google's highest-ranking executives.

In 1999, she began as Google's first marketing professional. Back then, she was responsible for a wide range of activities, including establishing the corporate identity and creating some of the first holiday logos. She also managed the licensing of Web search, site search, and enterprise to Google's first customers, and was responsible for the initial development of Google Image Search, Book Search, and Video Search. She now is Google's vice president of product management, responsible for Google's advertising, monetization, and measurement platforms products, including AdWords, AdSense, and Google Analytics.

Several of Susan's family members have worked at Google, including her husband. Dennis Troper is an operational executive. Eventually, Susan also became Sergey Brin's sister-in-law.

In less than a year, Google outgrew the garage. With eight employees, it moved into real office space on University Avenue in Palo Alto.

THE VENTURE CAPITALISTS

Stanford professor David R. Cheriton joined Yahoo!'s David Filo in urging Page and Brin to consider becoming entrepreneurs, but Cheriton went one step further. He hooked the Google boys up with an investor he knew.

Late one night in August 1998, Cheriton e-mailed Andy Bechtolsheim, a founder of Sun Microsystems and one of Silicon Valley's most successful venture capitalists. Bechtolsheim immediately responded, suggesting they

meet the next morning at eight o'clock. He passed
Cheriton's home on his way to work each day.

Cheriton, a Canadian-born and -educated computer
science professor, has become a billionaire as a result of
his investments in technology companies. Cheriton
co-founded Granite Systems with Andy Bechtolsheim, a
company that developed gigabit Ethernet products. Cisco
Systems acquired Granite in 1996. Cheriton later became
co-founder of Bechtolsheim's 2001 startup company,
Kealia, which was acquired by Sun Microsystems in 2004.

By the time he met Page and Brin, Bechtolsheim had
a lot of experience in starting companies. In addition to
his work with Cheriton, he was a co-founder of Sun
Microsystems. He knew his way around software, the
Internet, and Silicon Valley. Lounging in the morning
sun, Bechtolsheim watched Sergey and Larry's demo
for Google and immediately wrote a $100,000 check to
help launch the company.

Brin and Page celebrated the affirmation of their
work with breakfast at Burger King. "We thought we
should [eat] something that tasted really good, though it
was really unhealthy," Page said. "And it was cheap. It
seemed like the right combination of ways to celebrate
the funding."[5]

But there was a hitch. Bechtolsheim's check was
made out to Google Inc., a company that did not yet
legally exist. The check lay in Larry's desk drawer for

several weeks as he and Sergey set up a corporation under the Google name. They also sought other investors among family, friends, and acquaintances. Ultimately, they cobbled together a bankroll of $1 million.

Stage two of Google's financial evolution came on June 7, 1999—again, right in the middle of the Silicon Valley bubble-burst. Google got its second big push of funding from an unusual partnership of two leading venture capital firms, Sequoia Capital and Kleiner Perkins Caufield & Byers. Usually these two companies are fierce competitors, but in Google's case, it was different. Their representatives, John Doerr and Michael Moritz, both took seats on the board of directors, expertise that helped Larry and Sergey move the company rapidly in the right direction. Among other things, Doerr helped Sergey and Larry find their CEO, Eric Schmidt.

Doerr had an early career with Intel and moved into venture capital in 1980. He has directed essential funding to some of the most successful computer and Internet companies anywhere, including Compaq, Symantec, Sun Microsystems, Amazon, and Intuit.

Doerr says that several factors attracted him to Google. "You could see Google was growing rapidly," he said. Additionally, there was technical excellence; Larry and Sergey wanted to assemble a good management team. They were going after a very large market, and "they had a sense of urgency about them." And one particular characteristic that Doerr liked: "They were nerdy white males, dropouts with no social life."[6] Again, Larry and Sergey went off to Burger King to celebrate.

Only a year later, Google got its break when one of their professors and another Silicon Valley venture capitalist gave them startup money. That same year, articles praising the infant Google search engine appeared in *USA Today* and *Le Monde*. Soon, *PC* magazine named Google one of its Top 100 Web Sites and Search Engines.

While Doerr is one of the most influential denizens of Silicon Valley, he also has invested in failures. "John Doerr throws big darts at distant targets," said Jerry Kaplan, a Silicon Valley entrepreneur whose startups in the early 1990s, Go Corporation and Onsale.com, were flops backed by Kleiner through Doerr. "Most miss, but when they hit, it's spectacular."[7]

The Google investment was worth the risk. Kleiner Perkins and Sequoia Capital's $25 million got them 20 percent of Google back in 1999—as of November 2008, Google's market capitalization stood at about $108 billion.

THE ELUSIVE BUSINESS PLAN

The Google guys initially had a rough time coming up with a workable business plan. In 1999, the company was burning through its venture capital reserves without a clear strategy to generate revenues. It wasn't until early 2001 that they came up with the concept that would work.

As much as they disliked the idea, Larry and Sergey realized that advertising was a necessary part of their business model. Eventually, Google's management understood it had two core businesses, search and advertising. Search originally was a technology, not a business, but by servicing other sites, such as Yahoo! and AOL, it converted to a business. Search has gradually morphed into a portal as well, a website from which users can establish a home page, Gmail, and legions of other conveniences that connect them to the Internet but also keep them within Google. Advertising, every bit as complex and important as search, provides about 99 percent of Google's income.

Most Googlers now see the organization as a technology-driven media company. Google isn't so different from a magazine, newspaper, or television station. Content or programming, or in Google's case, search, is the lure. Advertising connected to the service provides the income. Many great fortunes, including those of Ted Turner, Michael Bloomberg, and Steve Forbes, have been built on advertising.

Nevertheless, as time went on, Google's business plan seemed more and more mysterious, even chaotic. Intel's Andy Grove has applauded *apparent* chaos as a way to obscure underlying intent, and if that is Google's goal, it has to some extent succeeded.

INVESTING IN WILD IDEAS

Google has tried to branch into, among other areas, a WiFi developer for cities, a major investor in renewable energy, green vehicles, and, strangest of all, a semi-biotech company, 23andMe. It is understandable when Google invests in any technology that broadens its ability to sell ads, and it may be smart to invest in cheaper electrical energy, since Google's business is so dependent on having a reliable power source. Genetic testing, however, doesn't seem to have any relationship to Google's core business.

Janet Driscoll Miller, president and CEO of Search Mojo, a search-engine marketing company, wrote: "23andMe was co-founded by Anne Wojcicki, new bride of Google's Sergey Brin, so the investment is likely driven more by nepotism than by the drive to build Google's business portfolio."[8]

Tom Foremski, who writes about business and culture in Silicon Valley, suggests that while Google's investment in such companies as 23andMe is legal, it may be unethical:

Investors cannot pressure Google to make money from those business groups because their shares carry minimal voting rights. Google's founders deliberately set up two classes of shares when they launched the public company, so that they could make decisions independent of shareholders (fellow owners) wishes.[9]

As it warned it would in the IPO prospectus, Google also expends a lot of energy and resources on high-risk products that don't always survive. National Public Radio *Marketplace* host, Kai Ryssdal, talked to *Fortune* magazine's Adam Lashinsky about Google's risk-and-failure strategy:

ADAM LASHINSKY: Yeah, you've gotta remember, this is a company that was started by two, 20-something-year-olds and from the beginning the Google cofounders nurtured a culture of both innovation on the one hand and chaos on the other hand. They were just gonna hang loose and play volleyball and go rollerblading and have massages on campus and make nifty stuff up. Well, that was tremendous once. But it isn't necessarily a proven way to build a business.

RYSSDAL: Seems to me what they have, actually, is very narrowly controlled chaos, which if you think about it is no way to run a billion-dollar business.

LASHINSKY: Well, narrowly controlled chaos—or managed chaos, which is what they call it—is exactly what they are trying to do. They want to encourage zaniness. On the other hand, they want to figure out *a way to control the zaniness. It's a radical concept. It's something everybody would like to do. You know, it's like work-life balance in our personal lives and careers. That's what they're trying to do in the shell of a $125 billion market-value company (in 2006).*

RYSSDAL: *All right, that's great. They've got this culture where anything goes and you can learn from your mistakes. Do you ever get fired, though, from Google? I mean, I've never heard of anybody losing their job there.*

LASHINSKY: *In fact, one of Google's most senior executives Sheryl Sanberg, who's a vice president and runs all of the automated advertising systems that Google has, told me about a multimillion-dollar mistake that she made. And when she realized her mistake she walked across the street at the Googleplex in Mountain View and she told cofounder Larry Page about it. What was interesting was his reaction. He said, "Yeah, we shouldn't have done that. We'll know better next time. But, oh, by the way, it's good that you made this mistake. I'm glad," he told her, "because we need to be the kind of company that is willing to make mistakes. Because if we're not making mistakes, then we're not taking risks. And if we're not taking risks, we won't get to the next level."*[10]

GOOD IDEAS PUT TO GOOD USE

While some of its corporate ventures seem off target, many of Google's charitable and public-spirited good works often feed into its business needs.

One such project was Google's student business plan competition in less-developed areas of the world. In 2007, students worked in teams to create a viable Internet business plan for Ukraine. The idea was to help support and grow Internet and online businesses in that country. The winning project, turned in by two students from the Institute of International Relations, was called "Interactive Tour Guide around Ukrainian Cities."

Similar competitions have been held in Africa and other regions. It is in Google's best interest to have more people online and surely surfing the Web using Google.

Additionally, Google.org, its philanthropic arm, invests millions of dollars in projects to develop cost-effective alternative energy sources, something Google dearly wishes for in order to keep its energy-gulping server farms running.

DEALING WITH DARK MATTER

When the 2008 recession hit, Google watchers were shocked to learn that the company would be laying off up to 10,000 employees, nearly half its workforce. Almost all of those at risk to go were contract workers.

"There is no question the number of workers is too high," said Brin.[11]

Eric Schmidt described the company's reaction to the economy as dealing with dark matter. Still, Google was in an excellent position to benefit from the global economic slump for several reasons:

- During such times, weaker companies disappear, and the strong, surviving companies either acquire the failing companies or seize their market share.
- Google had a large amount of cash on hand.
- According to some experts, online advertising may not be as strong as expected, but it will continue to grow. The marketing-research firm eMarketers predicted that Internet advertising would grow by 8.9 percent in 2008, as compared with the original prediction of 14.5 percent.
- Google can take the opportunity to fine-tune its product line, cherry picking the strong and potentially profitable projects and deleting those less likely to add significantly to the bottom line. Google immediately announced that it would drop its Lively-3D Avatars and Rooms, a virtual world, and Search Mash, an experimental search engine.

With a strong revenue stream and plenty of room to trim down, Google could emerge from economic hard times stronger and wiser.

AVERSION TO ADVERTISING

When they first started out, Page and Brin had a distaste for using advertising as the foundation for their business plan. In an academic paper that the two wrote while still at Stanford, they said that "advertising-funded search engines will inherently be biased toward the advertisers and away from the needs of consumers."[12]

It was several years before they changed their tune and accepted the fact that advertising was the only way to become a profitable commercial enterprise. Once they accepted the notion, they went forward with what soon became an extremely sophisticated advertising plan. The Google guys came to view advertising as an important service to consumers. "We look at ads as commercial information, and that goes back to our core mission of organizing the world's information," explains Omid Kordestani, vice president of Global Sales.[13]

To maintain their sense of integrity, advertising is always clearly identified as "sponsored links" at the top of the search listing, and Google does not accept pop-up advertising.

The simple text ads that appear at the top and in other places in Google search results account for almost all of the company's revenue. As an indication of how lucrative advertising is, in 2007 Google had annual revenues of $16.6 billion, with $4.2 billion of profit.

If all goes according to expectation, advertising revenues will only get better. Americans now spend an equal number of hours each week watching TV and surfing the Internet. Yet the Internet currently gets only a small percentage of the advertising dollars. Procter & Gamble, the largest advertiser in the United States, has an ad budget of $5.2 billion a year. Less than 2 percent of its measured ad budget is spent online; the vast majority is for television spots.

Yet large businesses may very well advertise on the Internet more and more. Online advertising is expected to grow at a 19.5 percent compound annual growth rate to $120 billion by 2012. By then, the Internet is expected to handle 19 percent of global advertising, compared with only 10 percent in 2007.[14]

Google ad revenues will grow both organically and by acquisition. In competition with Yahoo!, Microsoft, and the advertising-marketing giant WPP, Google bought the online advertising and marketing company DoubleClick. DoubleClick claims to handle about 12 billion transactions each day.

The $3.2 billion purchase of DoubleClick sparked complaints that Google was becoming too dominant in the advertising industry. It was such concerns that squelched a 2008 cooperative deal between Yahoo! and Google. (There is more on the Yahoo!-Google deal in the section "The Battle of Yahoo!" in the chapter "The Dominant Power in the Industry?")

That criticism has not slowed Google's expansion into other forms of advertising. It has marketed ads for newspapers, radio, and other traditional media. Despite its early dislike of advertising and claims that its business was purely search, even Eric Schmidt since has admitted, "We are in the advertising business."[15]

ADVERTISING THAT DELIVERS RESULTS

My light-bulb moment was where I realized that relevancy was king. I really saw it play out with Google . . . it was a big learning curve.[16]

—*Penry Price, Google's vice president for advertising
for North America*

The idea that advertising sells best when it is pertinent to search results helped Larry and Sergey come to terms with their business model, and it also delivered the economic payload. Advertisers liked the highly targeted ads, and searchers were more likely to click on an ad if it pertained to whatever they were thinking about when they typed words into the search box.

"I think the beauty of the search model is the one thing we know is your intent," explained Tim Armstrong, senior vice president for Google's North and Latin America advertising. "There's a chance that we're going to be able to give you the right information at the right time—the right ad to the right user at the right time with the right outcome—because it's a very self-directed form of advertising.

Google doesn't need to know who the end user is to be successful in advertising."[17]

Google was not the first Silicon Valley company to capitalize on the notion that relevancy mattered. Google's advertising approach was modeled after that used by GoTo.com, which allowed advertisers to bid to have a link to their website listed in the sponsored area whenever someone searched for certain key words. Rather than hire GoTo to handle its advertising, however, Google wrote its own software and adapted the GoTo model to its own uses.

GoTo was renamed Overture and sold to Yahoo!. Overture became a bitter rival from which Google seized the AOL advertising account. Yahoo! sued Google for copyright infringement, a dispute that was settled out of court. (For more information, go to the section "Lawsuits Everywhere" in the chapter "Google Grows Up.")

TWO WAYS TO ADVERTISE: ADWORDS AND ADSENSE

Google's advertising program has two distinct segments: AdWords, for those wishing to advertise a product or service, and AdSense, for websites wishing to get paid for displaying ads.

Launched in 2000, AdWords is Google's flagship advertising product and primary source of revenue. The pay-per-click advertising includes text and banner ads.

In the beginning, advertisers paid a set monthly fee for Google to set up and manage their campaigns. AdWords soon became something quite different—a self-service portal, a do-it-yourself tool that helped myriad small businesses get noticed.

In this second-generation service, advertisers bid both on words that should deliver their ads and on the maximum amount they are willing to pay per click. While the process is shrouded in mystery, one feature clearly appeals to advertisers. Google uses a Vickery auction system, in which winning bidders pay only one cent more than second-place bidders. This gives advertisers the courage to bid high, knowing that they will not be penalized if they are far above the market.

When a user Googles the bid-upon word, ads, also called *creatives* by Google, are shown as "sponsored links" at the top or on the right side of the screen. If the ad is appealing enough to inspire a searcher to click on it, the advertiser pays Google for every click.

The bid price helps get ads top placement on websites, but that is not the only factor. The ad can achieve top listing only if it appeals to enough Web surfers. The ad is assigned a "quality score." The quality score is calculated by historical click-through rates, relevance of an advertiser's ad text and keywords, an advertiser's account history, and other factors Google finds relevant. The quality score also has been used by Google to set the minimum bids for an advertiser's keywords. The minimum bid was meant to filter out low-quality ads, although there are reports that Google soon will drop the minimum bid.

"We literally buy millions of search terms," said Betsy Lazar, an advertising executive at General Motors, the nation's fourth largest advertiser. For example, "Chevy Detroit, Chevy, fuel-efficient vehicles."[18]

Suitcase designer Heys International built much of its business on Web advertising and has been highly successful, thanks to Google. "It's helped a lot of young innovative companies like ourselves get worldwide attention that we couldn't have gotten if it was [not] for search engines like Google," explained Heys founder, Emran Sheikh.[19]

Alice Bowe, a British garden designer, pays Google so that when anyone within 50 miles of her business types in "garden design," her site shows up. "I knew nothing about computers, or any of that sort of thing," she explained. "But it's really easy. You can type in as many different versions of the ad, and it will automatically try them out, then show the ones that do best more often."[20]

Google's Tim Armstrong points out, "We have customers that manage their individual ad campaigns every day, multiple times a day and improve them every day, multiple times a day."[21]

Beyond that basic service, Google then extended the ad-link concept so that websites automatically display ads linked to their text. AdSense technology can instantly analyze the text of any site and deliver relevant advertising.

Web-site owners use the AdSense program to earn money from text, image, and more recently, video advertisements on their websites. For many websites, AdSense is their main source of financial support. The advertisements are administered by Google and generate revenue on either a per-click or per-impression basis. The program has been a godsend for small websites that don't have the resources for hiring a sales staff and developing advertising sales programs.

A companion to the regular AdSense program, AdSense for Search allows the placement of the Google search box on websites. When a user searches the Internet or a website using the search box, Google shares any advertising revenue it makes from those searches with the website owner. However, the publisher is paid only if the searcher clicks on an ad on his page.

Google's advertising system is popular, but it isn't perfect. *Click fraud* has become a common practice, a subject that is explored in sections ahead.

AdWords has come under fire for allowing dvertisers to bid on trademarked keywords. In 2004, Google started allowing advertisers to bid on a wide variety of search terms in the United States and Canada, including the trademarks of their competitors, and in May 2008 expanded this policy to the United Kingdom and Ireland. Advertisers are restricted from using other companies' trademarks in their advertisement text if the trademark has been registered with Google's Advertising Legal Support team. Google requires certification to run regulated keywords, such as those related to pharmaceuticals, and some keywords, such as those related to gambling and hacking, are not allowed at all. These restrictions may vary by location.

Since June 2007, Google has banned AdWords' ads for student essay writing services, a move welcomed by university professors.

EXTENDING THE GOOGLE REACH

Google has been highly experimental when exploring the field of advertising. It ran a test in the *Chicago Sun Times*, selling box ads for newspapers. The program utilized "remnant space," unsold space where the paper otherwise would run house ads.

Google's YouTube is a huge success with users, but, so far, Google has not found a way to make money from the site. Video advertising could be the answer. Even as it was engaged in a lawsuit with Viacom, Google struck a deal to test inserting ads into video clips of Viacom programs. It also will run advertising along with some of CBS's primetime shows and soap operas.

Online video gamers, of whom there are about 200 million, may soon find lots of commercial spots on their favorite video games.

THE SCIENCE OF ADVERTISING

Google continues to develop features that help advertisers analyze and understand their target audiences, such as Google Insight for Search. This gimmick allows anyone to search on a word, product, service, and so forth, modify the search by geography, seasons, and other features, and then study the search patterns and volume for that subject. If the advertiser searches the word *chili*, for instance, and asks for results for the state of New Mexico, a graph appears showing that searches for the word *chili* peak every year in the autumn, exactly during the new chili harvest. She also can see that searches are the highest in the city of Albuquerque, although they also high in Texas. A chili merchant may have suspected that result, but now she knows for sure. It's a somewhat primitive tool in that the results aren't very detailed, but nevertheless it can be helpful to marketers.

GOOGLE DIDN'T ADVERTISE ITSELF—AT FIRST

"Google has built the most loyal audience on the web. And that growth has come not through TV ad campaigns but through word of mouth from one satisfied user to another." This is from Google's Corporate Information page, and the comment is true. At least Google never advertised itself in the traditional way, and its aversion to self-advertising may be dissolving.

Larry and Sergey sent out an e-mail in the spring of 1998, while Google was still in the development phase, to a list called Google Friends. "Google has now been up for over a month with the current database and we would like to hear back from you," they wrote. "How do you like the search results? What do you think of the new logo and formatting? Do the new features work for you? Comments, criticism, bugs, ideas . . . welcome. Cheers, Larry and Sergey."[22]

The word-of-e-mail seemed to work. People responded. Larry and Sergey sent out another e-mail in the summer: "Expect to see a lot of changes in Google in the next few months. We plan to have a much bigger index than our current 24 million pages soon. Thanks to all the people who have sent us logos and suggestions. Keep them coming. Have fun and keep Googling."[23]

Google also hired a market expert to come up with a plan for promoting itself. The plan would cost about half the money Google had on hand. Company leaders decided to pass. "Marketing would have killed the company," said Susan Wojcicki, "because we were going to spend like five or ten million dollars. We only had twenty million.

Imagine, you can cut us in half; suddenly we would have had to look for money or we would have had to do banner ads or something. We would not have had the luxury that we had later on."[24]

That isn't to say Google didn't spread the news about itself. From early in its life, Google promoted its search and search-ad products through distribution deals with software companies and by cross-promoting services like Gmail and Google Book Search with search ads and via its corporate blog.

Google also excelled at public relations. Early in its life, Google hired Cindy McCaffrey as director of public relations. She recommended a "press first" approach to promotion. By focusing on products and working with the media, Google would get plenty of free publicity in news stories.

By the spring of 2008, Google's growth had slowed to 39 percent, down from 58 percent a year earlier. In response to the slower growth, the company gradually began to shift its views on self-advertising.

Some Google employees apparently suggested promoting the company on NBC during the Olympics, but Sergey and Larry nixed the idea. However, in August of the same year, Google kicked off an ad campaign in Japan that included outdoor and online ads. The branding campaign was named "100 Things You Can Do With Google." Google did not advertise, but successfully placed dozens of stories in major media about its tenth birthday. Rumors flew that Google was talking with a New York advertising agency about an ad campaign in that city.

BIRTH OF THE GOOGLE ECONOMY

Google's search and advertising arrangements give Google both profits and power—if its algorithms demote your site, your visitors and your revenue will shrivel. As a result, an army of consultants has arisen who promise to push a website up the search rankings, or nudge anything negative off the all-important first page of results. The circle of search-optimization companies began to form around the enterprise and soon a satellite Google economy emerged.

Former Google go-fer Ginger Franke got the idea for her business, Franke Lifestyle Management (FLM), after Sergey hurt his back in a trapeze accident. She ordered a new mattress for him and went to his apartment to meet the delivery truck. She saw comic books on the shelves and a tattered futon and other personal details that helped her realize how little time entrepreneurs like Brin had to take care of their personal lives.

She got her on-the-job training for her business at Google. "In Franke's first years at Google, the company had as few as 50 employees and the pace was frenetic," wrote the *New York Times*, "so she quickly became a jack-of-all-trades, doing everything from filling bowls in the office with M&M's to planning company sales conferences that seemed to triple or quadruple in size each year."[25]

"These guys couldn't tell me how to do my job because they were too busy being entrepreneurs," said Franke, who previously worked at Netscape. "If I was going to survive, I would have to feel and not think."[26]

Eventually, Franke started FLM, an exclusive concierge service catering to Silicon Valley's high-tech high rollers.

—— Going Public ——

For companies, going public is a fundraising event. For the
cultures of those companies, it changes everything.[1]

—Marc Andreessen, who participated in the
initial public offerings of Netscape and
LoudCloud (now Opsware)

The initial public offering (IPO) has become a Silicon
Valley ritual, but like some ritualistic events (Christmas,
for example) it can get out of hand.

Larry and Sergey knew that a public stock offering
would change their personal lives. The world would
know how profitable Google had become and how
wealthy they had become as well. Their parents' and
their own lives would be in the spotlight, along with the
attendant pleasures and dangers of fame and wealth.

As Andreessen noted, everything the company does—
every quarterly and annual earnings statement, every

news release—will be scrutinized, and when actual information isn't available, gossip prevails. Additionally, many early, key employees become so wealthy that they gradually leave the company. They either don't need to work and go off to pursue personal dreams or they now can afford to start their own companies. In Google's IPO, more than half of the 1,000 mostly youthful employees were sure to become millionaires.

The freedom and fun of being privately owned is gone. Jeff Skoll, eBay's former president, recalls:

Before we went public, I used to send out a company-wide joke each day, just as a way of loosening things up. The day after the IPO, I sat down at my computer to write that day's joke and in walked the general counsel. He says to me, "You know that joke of the day thing? I think it's very funny." "Gosh, thank you," I replied. "Well, stop it," he said. "We are a public company now, and we don't want to offend anyone. If you want to keep sending out jokes, they can only be about lawyers." So I tried sending out lawyer jokes for two weeks—and then I gave up.[2]

Despite the downside, the Google boys knew that the time had come and they must take action. Their venture capitalists and private investors needed an IPO in order to get the expected return on their investment.

And Google itself could use the cash an IPO could raise to help it grow to its highest and best level.

But Larry and Sergey had become used to doing things their way, and the way they went public was no exception. True, they had reason to feel audacious. They had an advantage over other high-tech startups that tried floating themselves on the stock market. Google had been up and running for five years and had achieved profitability, although they had kept the company's dazzling profits from search-related advertising a secret thus far.

The stakes were high. Before the public offering, financial experts estimated that Google would be valued at $30 billion and that Larry and Sergey would be worth $4 billion each.[5] Finally on April 29, 2004, Google filed its S1, the required Securities and Exchange Commission (SEC) pre-IPO document.

Google's registration statement made a big splash. Many investors were on high alert for successful Silicon Valley companies formed by amazing young and creative minds. When they saw Google's strong revenues and profits, they suspected this might be the next one.

Google revealed that it had generated revenues of $961.9 million in 2003 and a net profit of $106.5 million. Sales rose 177 percent from 2002 although earnings increased by just 6 percent. Google also let it be known that it had been profitable since 2001 and was sitting on a war chest of a whopping $454.9 million in cash and cash equivalents.

But there were unsettling aspects to the offering as well, one of them being the earnest, seemingly naïve, and even arrogant "founder's letter" that accompanied the filing.

"WE'RE DIFFERENT"

It was an eye-opening piece of work, outlining an unconventional company with ambitious plans. Larry Page himself authored the letter, declaring that Google was different and intended to stay that way.

Page told prospective shareholders, "Google is not a conventional company. We do not intend to become one. Throughout Google's evolution as a privately held company, we have managed Google differently. We have also emphasized an atmosphere of creativity and challenge, which has helped us provide unbiased, accurate and free access to information for those who rely on us around the world."[4]

Google declared its independence from Wall Street in numerous ways, one of which was refusing to provide advance information to analysts on future financial performance. Google left Wall Street to figure it out for itself. "We don't provide guidance," declared Eric Schmidt. "We don't want to get in the way of running the business and guidance could limit that if they give quarterly lines."[5] Google would make all decisions for the best long-term interest of shareholders, even if quarterly earnings turned out to be bumpy.

Most shocking, the company named no chief executive officer, and the post would remain open until they got around to selecting one. Eric Schmidt would serve as chairman of the executive committee, giving him power over ceremonial and legal issues.

When the SEC first received Google's S1, the commission was not pleased. It asked for multiple changes to the papers, including a suggestion that the founders be less casual. "Throughout the document, you refer to executive officers, directors and principal shareholders by their first names," the SEC wrote. "For clarity, please consider revising the disclosure to refer to these persons by their full names or by their last names." Page and Brin refused to comply with the request.[6]

However, they did have to make some adjustments. At the time of the offering, the billion-dollar patent infringement lawsuit by Overture Services was already in the courts. The SEC wrote, "Your statement that the Overture Services lawsuit is 'without merit' is a legal conclusion, which Google is not qualified to make. Please revise [or] omit the statement."[7] This time Google complied, and then decided to settle the suit before going public. Google paid Yahoo! 2.7 million Google shares to use Overture's patented work.

THE DUTCH AUCTION

The IPO included another smackdown for Wall Street. Google would bypass investment bankers for the offering, using the Internet and an obscure *Dutch auction* process designed to draw a broader range of investors than the typical IPO. Page and Brin were deeply offended by the way investment bankers controlled who could buy shares, and often doled out purposefully underpriced IPO shares to insiders and preferred customers, who then sold the stock for a quick profit.

Google stock would be sold through brokerage houses, but anyone offering at or above the minimum bid could participate. Investors would be required to purchase at least five shares, an unusually low barrier of entry for this business.

Page explained why he and the management team chose the type of public offering they did:

> *Many companies going public have suffered from unreasonable speculation, small initial share float, and stock price volatility that hurt them and their investors in the long run. We believe that our auction-based IPO will minimize these problems, though there is no guarantee that it will.*[8]

As innovative as the idea was, it also brought risk. "The auction process for our public offering may result in a phenomenon known as the 'winner's curse,' and, as a result, investors may experience significant losses," warned Google.[9] This could happen if, caught up in the auction fervor, buyers bid too high for the shares, and in the hours, days, or weeks after the listing on the stock exchange, the share price collapsed.

The ever-skeptical columnist Allan Sloan wrote in *Newsweek*, "The real question is whether Google, like Buffett, will be able to ignore Wall Street's demands and go its own way. I doubt it . . . . Google will have to pay attention to its stock price—and thus, to Wall Street. I love the way that Google dissed the Street in its filing— distrusting the Street is the right move. Going public, I fear, will prove to be the wrong one."[10]

Google's form of ownership also was controversial. Page, Brin, and Schmidt set up a dual-class stock structure that allowed them to maintain control of the company. The three evoked the "1/10" rule, under which their B "supervoting" shares get 10 votes for every one vote allocated to an A share. In other words, the management triad together would cast 66.2 percent of the votes even though they owned only 31.3 percent of the company.

Page held 38.6 million shares, Brin, 38.5 million, and Schmidt, 14.8 million. The venture capital company Sequoia Capital held 23.9 million and Kleiner Perkins Caufield & Byers owned 23.9 million. John Doerr and Michael Moritz also had a piece of the action with 24 million shares each.

Among the advantages of the A/B share plan to the corporate leaders: Shareholders could not challenge controversial decisions and a hostile takeover would be impossible.

Subsequently, some shareholders—the Bricklayers & Trowel Trades International Pension Fund in particular—objected to the A/B share plan and forced a shareholder's proposal to void it. Obviously, without the management triad's support, the measure had no chance of passing.

BUFFETT ON GOOGLE

Master investor Warren Buffett had met Page and Brin at the Allen and Company's annual July conference in Sun Valley, Idaho. Then Larry and Sergey, along with Eric Schmidt, made a pilgrimage to Buffett's headquarters in Omaha, Nebraska, before Google went public.

All of this seems incongruous, considering that Buffett is best buddies with Google archrival Bill Gates of Microsoft and that Geico, an insurance company owned by Buffett's company, Berkshire Hathaway, was suing Google for trademark infringement at the time.

Yet Buffett was impressed with the two young men and their ideas. "It's not hard to see that Google is a phenomenal company," he said. "The whole idea of search never occurred to me. I never thought of it. Now at Geico we pay these guys a lot of money for this and that key word."*

The Google guys have a special combination of talents, he says. They understand both technology and business, and they know what the culture wants. "They've got a money sense that mixes with a culture sense."

Larry Page patterned his "Letter to Shareholders" in the annual report after the letter Buffett writes each year for Berkshire Hathaway.

*From author interview with Warren Buffett, December 10, 2008.

BERKSHIRE HATHAWAY'S SHARE STRUCTURE VERSUS GOOGLE'S

Brin once said that the A/B share structure was patterned after one used by Berkshire Hathaway and several major media corporations. In fact, the Google plan is nothing like the Berkshire plan, even though the end result may be similar.

Berkshire originally had only one class of shares, with Warren Buffett and his family holding the majority of those shares. When the Berkshire price rose to around $100,000 per share, some long-term shareholders complained that they would like to sell shares or distribute them as gifts, but the high stock price made that awkward. To resolve the matter and make the shares more liquid, Berkshire floated a new share offering of B shares that were worth 1/30 of an A share. An A share could be converted into 30 B shares. However, B shares had no voting rights and could not participate in an innovative charitable giving program, which since has been discontinued. So, even though Buffett continues to dominate the company on the basis of the large number of shares owned by him and his family members, he is not the only one who can own A shares. All A shares carry exactly the same voting rights that Buffett does. Anyone can still buy A shares, and anyone who chooses to do so can buy B shares.

Morgan Stanley and Credit Suisse First Boston became Google's lead banks, and the company picked NASDAQ as its exchange, trading under the symbol GOOG.

Snubbing fate again, the Google guys chose the month of August for the IPO, a time when most of Wall Street traditionally packs it in and goes to the beach. Scarier yet, they picked Friday the 13th to list their shares. The company announced it would sell $2,718,281,828 worth of its shares—another little Google/mathematician joke. The seemingly random number is the numerical definition of *e*, a concept something like *pi*, and a familiar concept to math geeks. At first, Google set a price range of $108 to $135 per share. Later, due to roiling controversy, the initial share price was trimmed to $85 per share. Most companies structure the offering so they can go public around $20 a share.

On the day the shares went on sale, the price rose to $100 and by the next day shares were trading at $108.31. By 2008, the shares soared to $741.79 before the 2008 recession caused the shares to plummet more than 60 percent. Even then, the shares never dropped below $247.

Google showed an independent streak in its approach to the IPO, but it also got badly knocked around during the process. On May 4, just days after the going-public announcement, the insurance giant Geico filed a lawsuit against the search engine for trademark infringement for selling its name as a search word. This cast a cloud on the proceedings since Google had lost similar lawsuits in France and Germany.

The SEC also took a close look at Google's books and found irregularities. In 2003, the company had issued vast numbers of shares and options without registering them or informing employee shareholders of its financial results. The company was forced to correct the error by buying back the shares. It was never clear why this had happened, but speculation was that it came about because of Sergey and Larry's fondness for secrecy.[11]

THE *PLAYBOY* INTERVIEW

Amidst all the controversy and confusion, Larry and Sergey made another misstep. Once the registration statement was filed with the SEC, Google would be in the required *quiet period* until the stock actually sold. During this time, the company was prohibited from doing or saying anything that would hype the shares.

In April, just a month before they would be filing for the IPO and entering the SEC-mandated quiet period, they granted an interview to *Playboy* magazine. Clearly there was risk that the article would appear before the IPO was complete. When the story came up in an issue of the girly rag, questions again arose as to the founders' maturity. While the story didn't run until the September 2004 issue, copies of the magazine usually are available or on newsstands long before the publication date. Thus, the "candid conversation" did become public during the silent period. Again, it seemed as if the IPO might be interrupted. But after weeks of worry and scrambling by Google's attorneys, the SEC agreed to allow the story to be listed as an addendum to the S1, making it formally part of the full disclosure requirement.

It helped settle stormy waters when all three top executives—Larry Page, Sergey Brin, and Eric Schmidt—in the runup to the IPO reduced their annual salaries to a dollar a year and refused bonuses, tying their personal wealth directly to the company's performance in the stock market. Google was back on track to be one of the most unique and unlikely IPOs in the history of Wall Street.

In the end, those strong earnings, profits, and reserve funds prevailed and the Google guys pulled it off. The initial public offering took place on August 18, 2004, with 19,605,052 shares selling at an opening price of $85 per share. Google's offering raised $1.67 billion, giving the company a market capitalization of $23 billion. A number of Google employees with shares in the company became millionaires overnight, and Larry Page and Sergey Brin found themselves multibillionaires at age 27. Google was an immediate favorite with individual investors and the stock price has soared.

One of the big winners from Google's public offering was Stanford University, which actually owns key Google technology developed at the University. When the IPO was complete, Stanford held 7,574 shares of Class A and 1,650,289 shares of Class B Google. According to the SEC, those holdings were valued at $179.5 million. Stanford trustees sold 184,207 shares, netting a quick $15.6 million.

TEN YEARS LATER

Google entered 2008, the tenth anniversary of its founding, with trumpets blaring and triumphant flags flapping in the breeze:

- Month-by-month its share of the search market was growing at well over 15 percent annually, reaching nearly 60 percent early in the year.

- Its financial position was like a fortress, with $14.2 billion in cash, $17.3 billion in assets, and only $2.4 billion in current liabilities.
- In the four years after going public, sales revenues had rocketed from $3.2 billion to $16.6 billion. Net income had increased even more, going from $399 million in 2004 to $5.3 billion at the end of 2007.
- Google now had a workforce of nearly 20,000 compared to 3,000 four years earlier.
- The company was acquiring new businesses such as YouTube and pioneering products in all sorts of fields, including the storing of medical records and other information online.

Even so, there were signs that the Google phenomenon had reached a new phase, and that perhaps expectations for "the search engine that could" had become overblown.

Google was beginning to scare people with its unbelievable reach into privacy, property rights, and human rights. Its competitors were feeling the hot breath of Google on their necks in dozens of Internet and wireless realms. The company was accused of wanting to dominate all forms of advertising, concerns that scuttled a proposed advertising partnership with Yahoo!. *BusinessWeek* posed the question, "Is Google too powerful?," and *Wired* magazine declared, "Who's Afraid of Google? Everyone."

Writing for The Motley Fool website, Alyce Lomax admitted that Google was an innovative and smart company, but she had her doubts about the long term. "Here's why I'm apathetic to all the Google hoopla: Its other products haven't come anywhere near its success with core Internet Search (and lucrative targeted advertising). Fortunately for it, that financial success has allowed it to carry on like an abstract artist/prima donna, throwing a bunch of stuff against the wall to see what sticks. But so far, it has been impressive just how little these extras have really mattered to Google."[12]

The Economist speculated that Google's share price had peaked at $742 on November 6, 2007, a suspicion that would be confirmed in the months to come (at least so far). The stock's first real slide could be partly blamed on a touchy stock market, but also partly on a slight slowing in Google's miraculous growth.

In early 2008, the shares took a second pounding when some market analysts predicted that Google's ad sales would decline substantially. On February 28, 2008, the shares fell $10.8 billion in market capitalization in just 20 minutes. When the sales numbers came out, Google defied the rumors, still running strong. The share price recovered somewhat, but still closed 25 percent from its January high.

Not long after, the realization of a worldwide recession clenched the markets in fear and Google soon lost

60 percent of its value. At one point in the year, Google traded as low as $247. By the autumn of 2008, Page and Brin had lost roughly half of their net worth (a total of $12.1 billion) due to volatility in the stock market.

It was true that Google's breakneck-speed growth had slowed a little, but the results were still darn good. Third-quarter profits grew a healthy 26 percent, although they paled somewhat compared to 35 percent in the third quarter of 2007. The number of third-quarter paid advertising clicks grew by 18 percent, off only slightly from 2007's 19 percent.

To Google's credit, the company did not go into denial. Sergey admitted the company was as vulnerable to economic strife as any other:

> *To the extent that everybody starts spending a lot less, I don't think we are necessarily immune. I don't think any company is immune to a total bust.*[13]

Although Eric Schmidt said he was optimistic about Google's future, he added, "We are in uncharted waters now."[14]

The company immediately began reviewing all of its expenditures, including the hours of free cafeteria service and liberal building of data centers. Google began reducing its army of 10,000 contract employees. Schmidt said he would trim away any program the company was merely "fiddling with."[15]

It wasn't entirely bad news at Google, though. The preparation for hard times came early and Google's financial footing has remained solid. Its percentage of the search business kept growing, and along with it, ad sales. "Google just continues to grab market share," said Matt Tatham, spokesman for the market research company Hitwise. "There's no ceiling for them."[16]

Three months after Google's tenth anniversary and in the midst of much gloom, The Motley Fool's Alyce Lomax now saw Google's belt-tightening as positive. "On Google's 10-year anniversary in September, I said that its creativity needs to be tempered with maturity and restraint. Maybe the company finally gets it. Or maybe tough times build character in companies and people alike. Whatever the case, a grown-up Google could end up becoming a very good thing for investors' long-term portfolios."[17]

The Vision

Larry and Sergey's deep sense of purpose drove Google from the beginning: "Sergey and I founded Google because we believed we could provide an important service to the world—instantly delivering relevant information on virtually any topic," wrote Larry Page in Google's first corporate report.

> *Serving our end users is at the heart of what we do and remains our number one priority. Our goal is to develop services that significantly improve the lives of as many people as possible. We are proud of the products we have built, and we hope that those we create in the future will have an even greater positive impact on the world.*[1]

Google aspires "to create designs that are useful, fast, simple, engaging, innovative, universal, profitable, beautiful, trustworthy and personable. Achieving a harmonious balance of these ten principles is a constant challenge. A product that gets the balance right is 'Googley'—and will satisfy and delight people all over the world."

~

"Larry and Sergey thought a lot about [our mission] before they got started," explained Google Vice President Marissa Mayer. "At other companies, there are these Dilbertian crews of HR people who show up and say: 'We've outgrown our mission and we need to write a new one.' That has never happened at Google. The mission is exactly what Larry and Sergey wrote back in the fall of 1998, before any of us were even here."

Despite frequent early statements that Google was about search, Mayer said that the vision always was broader than that. "It wasn't just about Web search. When I showed up, I said, 'Guys, shouldn't we be calling the company Google. com?' They said: 'Oh, we're not just a dot.com. We're not going to be just about the Web. We're going to be all kinds of things.'"[2]

~

In the fall of 2004, Google's top management realized they needed more structure. They engaged in a process of strategic review, or "visioning" about the company meaning, intent, and future. It all started when Page and Brin went into all-night seclusion, writing what became known as "The Tablets." (To read the Google Ten Commandments, check out the section "Ten Things Google Has Found to Be True," in the chapter "Google Culture.")

MAKE IT USEFUL

Google is my rapid-response research assistant. On the run-up to deadline, I may use it to check the spelling of a foreign name, to acquire an image of a particular piece of military hardware, to find the exact quote of a public figure, check a stat, translate a phrase, or research the background of a particular corporation. It's the Swiss Army knife of information retrieval.[3]

—*Garry Trudeau, cartoonist and creator,*
"Doonesbury"

Page and Brin felt from the beginning that they should work on something that was not simply theoretical, but that would be helpful to others. Their dreams combined several possible careers into one. "My goal was to work on something that was academically real and interesting," Page recalls.

From an early age, I also realized I wanted to invent things. So I became really interested in technology . . .

and business. So probably from when I was 12 I knew
I was going to start a company eventually.

Google teams take the mission a step further, trying to discover needs that people don't yet know they have.

There is no question that Google is useful and the ways in which it can be useful seem endless. For example, a bicyclist in the 2008 Olympics described how she used Google Earth to study the Olympic bicycle route in China and then find a similar route in the United States on which to practice. Land surveyors are using Google Earth for preliminary job-site reconnaissance and for planning the survey. During the 2008 elections, Google used its maps to create a website to help voters find their polling places. The list of ways to use Google goes on.

Some ideas seem useful but don't turn out that way. The "I'm Feeling Lucky" button directs users to the first page Google returns for their query. So, where did the idea for a button that anticipates exactly what someone wants work out?

During a National Public Radio *Marketplace* interview, Sergey explained, "The reason it's called 'I'm Feeling Lucky,' is of course that's a pretty damn ambitious goal. I mean to get the exact right one thing without even giving you a list of choices, and so you have to feel a little bit lucky if you're going to try that with one go. That's one of the other problems with the button. It doesn't always take you where you want to go. But since it's there, surely people must be using it."

Marisa Mayer, Google's vice president responsible for everything on the search page, says not really. It's not a popular item. "I would say it's less than 1 percent of our searches are done through the 'I'm Feeling Lucky' route," she said. Even Sergey Brin admits, "I sometimes use it, though rarely."

Tom Chavez heads Rapt, a company that helps determine the dollar value of advertising on a Web page. He did the math on how much the 1 percent of people who use the button are costing the company. "Basically," says Chavez, "you have $110 million of revenue loss per year associated with that button."[5] The loss comes because of the advertising that searchers don't get a look at. Google keeps the button, however, because of what it sees as a comfort factor.

THE MANY WAYS TO GOOGLE

There are scores of ways to use Google, and creative applications are added so quickly it's nearly impossible to keep track.

Simple searches on Google (as well as many other search engines) have become ridiculously easy. The search box also acts as:

- **A calculator:** Insert any equation, such as $56 \times 287 \div 11$, and get a quick result.

- **A converter:** Miles to kilometers, pints to gallons, kilograms to pounds—ask and you'll get the answer.

- **A cook book:** Go to your refrigerator, check the leftovers, odds and ends, and so on. Type the items into the Google text box and come up with a recipe. The day after Thanksgiving, the items "avocado, orange, turkey, cranberry, cheese," brought up search results of a recipe for turkey tacos with cranberry salsa. Yummy!

- **A telephone directory:** Type in the word *phonebook*, a colon, a name, and a location, and get the number. If you want to track down your old college roommate, Slym Smyth, and you think he's in Miami, type in phonebook:slym smyth Miami FL and the number should come up. This feature offers an "opt-out" button. Remove your name from the phonebook if you wish.

- **A stock ticker:** The symbol GOOG links to a real-time share price for the company. It works for any stock. All you need is a company's stock exchange symbol.

- **A flight tracker:** Type in the flight number, such as AA 377, and track a flight's progress.

- **A ride finder:** If you want to move around one of ten major U.S. cities, this is a taxi, limousine, and shuttle search service using real-time positions of vehicles.
- **Another chance:** If you hit a brick wall with your search, or do not turn out to be lucky at all, explore Banana Slug (www.bananaslug.com). Banana Slug was developed as an application program interface (API) to Google. At the site you key in your search words, select a category for your search, and then hit the search button. Banana Slug adds a random word from your chosen category. Often this random category word brings up an entirely new list of hits where you may find the one you're seeking.

Google applications cover an extensive range of tasks and subjects. Some are appropriate for typical computer users. Others are for more sophisticated Web-oriented individuals.

- **Chrome browser:** Designed to compete with Microsoft and Firefox, Chrome recently emerged from the beta stage as a simple but very fast browser with some unusual features.
- **Documents and Spreadsheets:** This free software is similar to, but less sophisticated than, that sold by Microsoft. The software also allows the sharing of information in real time.
- **Flights SMS:** For mobile phone users, this delivers information on the status of your flight when you

text your airline and flight number to 4666453 (GOOGLE).

Google Android: Software platform and operating system for mobile phones.

Google Books: Selects books according to search keyword, then allows browsing of certain volumes and the download of full text of others. For example, the Shakespeare search feature lets users locate classic texts from the Bard of Avon.

Google Earth: Images of Earth and even the galaxies with 360-degree views. The images aren't real-time, and if you zoom in too close they get fuzzy, but it's a cool tool. Google also offers views of the ocean floor.

I Feel Lucky: A seldom-used Google feature, I Feel Lucky takes searchers directly to the top search result, sans advertising. Google keeps the button in place as a comfort to users.

Google Images: If you're just curious about the available photos of celebrities, from Alaska Governor Sarah Palin to actor Matt Damon to sports figures, go to Google Images. There are images of all types—drawings, paintings, cartoons, posters, and more. Easy to borrow (or steal or sample) for your own art projects.

Google Maps: Gives maps and directions to specific addresses. Other features have been integrated into the maps, including public transportation routes, and locations of schools, museums, and so forth.

Gmail: Not the first or even the best e-mail service, but probably the one with the largest storage capacity. Gmail users also get advertisements linked to keywords in the messages.

Google News: An aggregator of news summaries from 4,500 English-language news sources, the service can be customized according to the user's interests.

Google Sets: In the Google window, type in Google Sets. Up pops an application that allows you to start a list of a certain collection of things; then Google gives you a longer list of like items. For example, type in ruby, opal, emerald, and you'll get an inventory of precious stones. Enter common garden flowers such as rose, violet, daisy, and a list of domesticated flowers appears. By contrast, type in yarrow, lupine, harebell, and the list is completed with wildflowers. This is a useful tool for jogging the memory or adding more information to what you already know.

Google Street: Photographs of actual streets and even specific addresses in most U.S. cities and many other cities around the world. This application tends to make residents fairly nervous.

Google Talk: An alternative to the telephone, this allows you to speak to people anywhere, anytime, using a computer.

Voice Local Search: Free service from any telephone. Call 1-800-GOOG-411 (1-800-466-4411) and ask for a business by name or type and location. A pleasant male voice responds, and entertains with scat singing while the information is retrieved.

YouTube: Social networking website featuring video clips and some full television shows. It's free, but you may discover ads appearing with certain videos.

MAKE IT BIG

"Google's ambition," explained Eric Schmidt, "is to solve big problems that impact a lot of people."[6] Schmidt adds that the Google guys "think about what should be and assume it is possible."[7]

"Solving big problems is easier than solving little problems," claims Larry.[8] One reason Google sponsors its annual Zeitgeist conference is to encourage those attending to think about solutions to the world's major dilemmas.

~

In one strategy meeting, Brin and Page were annoyed at the presentation. Page complained that the engineers weren't ambitious enough. Brin agreed, calling the proposals muddled and overly cautious. "We want something big," said Page. "Instead you proposed something small. Why are you so resistant?"[9]

Google officially became the world's largest search library in 2000, one with a billion-page index. By mid 2008, its engineers reported that they had registered the trillionth Web page into the search engine.

We Serve the World

We continue our efforts to make Google more global. Google is available in 160 different local country domains and 117 languages (including some obscure ones like "Swedish Chef"— Bork, Bork, Bork).

—*Google's 2007 Annual Report*

The first ten foreign-language versions of Google.com were released in 2000, with access in French, German, Italian, Swedish, Finnish, Spanish, Portuguese, Dutch, Norwegian, and Danish. Those who speak Afrikaans to Icelandic to Zulu can now use Google in their native tongues.

Checking out Google's language list, you might find yourself wondering where Twi is spoken. In addition to Bork, Bork, Bork (the language of the Swedish chef from the Muppet Show), those conversant in fictitious tongues such as Klingon and Elmer Fudd also can Google: " . . . lots of people use our services in places Sergey or I haven't been to yet," Page noted.

While Google offers a service that hooks up translators with those needing translations, one of Google's most challenging and intriguing projects is automated, machine-based language translations. Instead of converting to a new language the traditional way, the system searches for the most often and commonly used translation of words and phrases. Then it puts them together in sentences. So far the translations are fairly crude, but language experts believe that with Google's huge database, this kind of translation should become smoother over time.

According to Eric Schmidt, "We will eventually do 100 by 100 languages, to take this set of languages and convert to another. This alone will have a phenomenal impact on an open society."[10]

~

Google opened its first office outside the United States in 2001. Seven years later, the company operated more than 60 offices abroad. Google knows that the Internet is for the most part oblivious to international borders, and increasingly, the actual world is becoming more like the virtual world. "We strive to be a local company in every country that we operate [in] and we understand that our users all have different cultures," says Google.

When Google went into South Korea and China, it had to alter its minimalist home page. Web surfers there preferred pages that were visually complex and offered a lot of entertainment.[11]

Google is still working to establish business presences in places such as the Middle East. "As we expand our operations and hire our first employees in another country, that part of Google feels like a startup," wrote Larry Page in the 2007 Annual Report. "Every time we travel to a new Google office we see amazing, smart, excited people and lava lamps," Page said.[12]

Attention to global markets makes good business sense: By 2008, more than half of Google's revenue was coming from outside the United States.[13]

~

"It turns out the real world matters to people, in the form of maps, satellite images, business locations, bike paths, and all other types of geographic data. We are hard at work in all these domains."[14]

Google also literally goes out of this world with Sky mode—a dazzling view of the night sky, complete with super-high-resolution images from the Hubble telescope.

MAKE IT FUN

Google has improved my sex life, tightened my abs, and brought me closer to God. (I keed.) Actually, as a working gossip columnist, I appreciate Google as a rough—very rough—research tool. The Internet is still the Wild West.[15]

—*Lloyd Grove, columnist,* New York Daily News

Silicon Valley has a history of April Fools' Day jokes, and Google joins right in. In 2000, Google announced the MentalPlex, Google's ability to read your mind as you visualize the search results you are seeking. Sometimes the April Fools' Day jokes get jumbled up with more serious business. On April 1, 2004, Google proclaimed it would open a research facility on the moon. On the same day, it announced its Web-based, free mail service, Gmail. Shooting for the moon clearly was a prank, but what about Gmail? It was real.

~

Google has tried to infuse a sense of fun into its hunt for greater advertising revenues. This was most apparent when it made itself a liaison between Hollywood talent and online entertainment with its "Seth MacFarlane's Cavalcade of Cartoon Comedy" project. The clips of the television show *The Family Guy* were offered to a number of Web pages frequented by 18- to 34-year-old men. "We can work with more and more Seths and connect them to advertisers," said Alexandra Levy, director of branded entertainment at Google.[16]

Larry Page is impressed by the entertainment available on his own website: "I'm amazed at the quality and diversity of the video available on Google Video, with more being added every day. You can buy first-run programs, such as *Survivor* from CBS, with high picture quality, and watch them on your computer anytime." Page marveled that users could submit their own videos and let anyone in the world watch them for free or embed a video from Google Video on any Web page:

> *To view some of my favorites, search for "Russian climbing" for acrobatics on tall buildings, "bsb" for amazing lip synchers, or "airbus 7" to watch an Airbus being built in seven minutes.*[17]

~

Sports fans get in on the action, too. In 2008, Google provided Street View for the entire Tour de France bicycle race route, the first launch of Street View imagery in Europe.

~

Sometimes the fun-loving business style at Google seems just plain juvenile. In 2006, Brin, Page, and Schmidt were preparing for a Google sales conference at the massive San Francisco Moscone Center. Beforehand, they met with a *Time* reporter, Adi Ignatius. The group gathered at a table covered with Lego bricks. The story that Page once built a printer out of Legos has become legendary. Both Brin and Page were busy snapping bricks together. Ignatius asked what they were building. "I was hoping to build a Lego nuclear reactor," said Brin, "but I think I have a bazooka-wielding robot." Page chimed in, "Hey, I know. Let's build Eric out of Legos."

Later the reporter asked how the management team was dealing with the need for transparency in their business. Brin held up a clear plastic piece, "Look, I'm only using transparent Legos."[18]

Google Users Hearken to the Call

If Googlers don't make the website Googly enough, those using Google will add their own enhancements. Internet searchers have compiled a list of amazing sights from Google Earth. They have discovered that from on high the gardens at Chateau de Versailles look like a giant, grinning puppy. Hiding in the hills of Alberta, Canada, is the image of an enormous native American, complete with headdress. And a likeness of Jesus can be found in Peruvian sand dunes.

To make the planet even more alluring, humans have started creating art that can be seen from space, if some of it can be called "art." Kentucky Fried Chicken's Colonel Saunders has been painted into the Nevada desert, Oprah Winfrey fans put her face in a farm field, and if you're still wondering where Waldo is, his oversized image has been painted on rooftops here and there around the globe.

~

Before anyone gets too silly, the company warns, "Google doesn't let fun or personality interfere with other elements of a design, especially when people's livelihood, or their ability to find vital information, is at stake."[19]

DON'T DO EVIL

Management is doing things right; leadership is doing the right things.[20]

—*Peter F. Drucker*

In the 2004 *Playboy* interview that played havoc with its public offering process, the writer asked whether "Don't Do Evil" was truly the company motto.

"Yes, it's real," insisted Sergey.

"Is it a written code?" asked the reporter.

"Yes," said Sergey. "We have other rules too." He added, "It's not enough not to be evil. We also actively try to be good."[21]

In 2001, Google engaged its employees in an exercise of defining the company and setting goals. The company's engineers, notoriously anti-corporate, *pooh-pooh*ed the discussion. But one engineer, Paul Buchheit, spoke the words that many were thinking. Buchheit said that all the ideas kicking around could be wrapped up in the phrase, "Don't be evil." The statement resonated and stuck.

David Friedberg, who left Google to found Weather-Bill, which helps companies protect themselves from damaging weather events, said that before every acquisition, the pair asked whether it could be evil. "That was always the consideration," he said.[22]

Bret Taylor, who became a venture capitalist after exiting Google, said that the founders' attention to the slogan made him feel part of something special. "They always made me feel much bigger than myself."[23]

How Google Defines *Evil*

Eric Schmidt once quipped that evil was whatever Sergey Brin said it was. Google's experiences show how difficult it is to pin down the definition of *evil*.

Brin says that there often is discussion about the definition of *evil* and how not to be evil. "We deal with all varieties of information," he says.

Somebody's always upset no matter what we do. We have to make a decision, otherwise there's a never-ending debate. Some issues are crystal clear. When they're less clear and opinions differ, sometimes we have to break a tie. For example, we don't accept ads for hard liquor, but we accept ads for wine. It's just a personal preference. We don't allow gun ads, and the gun lobby got upset about that. We don't try to put our sense of ethics into the search results, but we do when it comes to advertising.[24]

When *Mother Jones* magazines asks, "Is Google Evil?," the discussion has become serious.[25] "When faced with doing the right thing or doing what is in its best interests, Google has almost always chosen expediency," wrote *Mother Jones*.[26]

As evidence, the magazine cited the incidents where Google eliminated links to an anti-Scientology site after the Church of Scientology claimed copyright infringement. In another instance, Google apparently handed over some records of social networking sites on the service Orkut to the Brazilian government. Yet, the Church of Scientology had a legitimate legal claim, and the Brazilian government was operating within its own laws in investigating alleged racial, homophobic, and pornographic content.

Google's website explains that the company will remove pages that violate U.S. law or the law of a host country, or breach its own Webmaster Guidelines.

One blogger said, "While I do not consider Google 'evil' (I reserve that label for really bad things in life), I do think that they are the big bully on the block."[27]

From privacy to property rights to human rights, the scope and influence of Google have led to unintended consequences, some of them tragic:

- Google has come under fire for borrowing patented or copyrighted material without permission, and for allowing AdWords advertisers to bid on trademarked keywords.

- A video was posted on Google's Italian-language site showing four high school boys humiliating another young man with Down's syndrome.
- Courts in Mumbai, India, were considering whether terrorists used Google Earth to help plot attacks in that city that left 170 dead and many more injured.

There are numerous areas in which Google clearly takes the moral high ground:

- Google requires certification to run regulated keywords, such as those related to pharmaceuticals and other legal drugs. Some keywords, such as those related to gambling and hacking, are not allowed at all.
- From June 2007, Google banned AdWords ads for student essay writing services. While most universities welcomed the move, there is no restriction on such sites appearing in the regular Google search results.
- In an idea that is at the same time informative and peculiarly spooky, Google studied searches on cold, flu, and pain treatments and medications to help identify areas where flu epidemics are occurring.

The Motto Loses Some Shine

In the beginning, everyone was impressed and even touched by the notion that a young company would so diligently guard against bad behavior in its own ranks. Then as Google grew like Man in the Moon Marigolds, the questioning began.

"Apparently a certain percentage of any set group of people looks for signs that companies with sterling reputations are actually fronting for Satan," writes a former Googler on his website. "And of course, with Google's 'Don't be evil' motto hanging on its back like a 'kick me' sign, the company got cut very little slack."[28]

Amazon CEO and Google investor Jeff Bezos observed: "Well, of course, you shouldn't be evil. But then again, you shouldn't have to brag about it either."[29]

~

Google executives, claim some observers, have been slowly edging away from the company's famous pledge. Vice President Marissa Mayer sounded a retreat from the motto when she declared that "Don't Be Evil" never was and never would be an elected or ordained motto.

"'Don't be evil' is misunderstood," said Eric Schmidt in a 2008 interview. "We don't have an evil meter . . . the rule allows for conversation. I thought when I joined the company this was crap . . . it must be a joke. I was sitting in a room in the first six months . . . talking about some advertising . . . and someone said that it is evil. It stopped the product. It's a cultural rule, a way of forcing the conversation, especially in areas that are ambiguous."[30]

Can Free Speech Go Too Far?

Putting the word "Jew" into the Google search box at one time instigated a scorching debate on the subject of ethics, morality, fairness, and unintended consequences. When Steven Weinstock, a New York real estate investor and former yeshiva student, searched on the word "Jew," he was horrified at the results. An aggressively anti-Jewish website called "Jew Watch" came up at the top of his search list. Weinstock went on a crusade, circulating an online petition demanding that Google remove the site from its index.

The dilemma is both painful and common: Free speech clearly is the mark of an open and democratic society, but instigating hate against any group of people is both wrong and dangerous. As unlikely as it may seem, charges floated on the Internet that Google was anti-Semitic and had purposely placed a hate-site high in its rankings.[31]

Google did not remove the offensive site from its index, but apparently, for a while, included a tag at the top of the search warning people that Jew Watch contained offensive material. Some observers claim that

Google now has partially blocked the site. A recent search of the word "Jew" in Google did not bring the site up, even far down the list. However, a search of the words "Jew Watch" did locate the site, and it appeared without the offensiveness warning.

Google offers this perspective:

> *If you use Google to search for "Judaism," "Jewish," or "Jewish people," the results are informative and relevant. So why is a search for "Jew" different? One reason is that the word "Jew" is often used in an anti-Semitic context. Jewish organizations are more likely to use the word "Jewish" when talking about members of their faith. The word has become somewhat charged linguistically, as noted on websites devoted to Jewish topics such as these.*[32]

Not all Jewish people object to being labeled as Jews, and not all believe that Google should block the site. "Some responsibility for this needs to rest on our own shoulders," said Jonathan Bernstein, a regional director of the Anti-Defamation League, "and not just a company like Google. We have to prepare our kids for things they come across on the Internet. This is part of the nature of an Internet world. The disadvantage is we see more of it and our kids see more of it. The advantage is, we see more of it, so we're able to respond to it. I'm not sure what people would want to see happen. You couldn't really ask Google not to list it."[33]

~

GoogleWatch wrote: "It's not that we believe Google is evil. What we believe is that Google Inc. is at a fork in the road, and they have some big decisions to make."[34]

(For more on the debate regarding right and wrong, see the chapter "Google Grows Up.")

MAKE IT FREE

Google has a history of entering businesses in which other companies are engaged, but offering the service free. This is possible, due to the colossal revenues Google collects from relevant advertising. "Frankly," says Eric Schmidt, "the free service model with free advertising is still the best model."[35] The advertising itself isn't free, of course, but it is reasonable.

Over time, Google has challenged almost all the major players in the software and Internet world, and truly frightened the competitors with the freebies. Google's productivity programs, which operate from the Web, are a direct attack on Microsoft. Microsoft isn't the only company that feels compelled to take a defensive stance where Google is concerned. Google Base—a collection of software—threatened craigslist, eBay, Monster, and

Tribe.net. Google Books frightens authors, publishers, bookstores, and especially Amazon.

Some of the complimentary programs don't seem to have much impact. Google offered a free coupon program to its advertisers, linked to product and services searches using Google Maps. Few companies use the service.

In many cases it isn't clear why Google is offering the no-charge services. Google Voice Local Search, activated by calling toll-free 1-800-GOOG-411, has no apparent advertising attached. At best, it seems like an experiment in voice-activated search.

Even so, Google's cost-free programs create buzz and goodwill. Just in time for the 2008 Beijing Olympics, Google announced a music search and download service in China—free, of course.

— Google Culture —

Company cultures are like country cultures. Never try to change one. Try, instead, to work with what you've got.[1]

    —Peter Drucker, late author and management guru

The Google website proclaims that although the company has grown rapidly, it maintains a small-company feel. That is wishful thinking. Googleplex is a colorful, compelling campus, but with its dozens of buildings spread over a half-dozen city blocks, it is anything but intimate.

When asked how Google had changed since its inception, Director of Technology Craig Silverstein said: "I used to know everyone at the company and now I do not. It makes me sad."

Google is supported by workers in scores of offices around the United States and the world. The Santa Monica office definitely has the look and feel of a branch office. There is nothing cozy about the European head-quarters in Dublin—two high-rises in an industrial area. Given the website's achievements, it was bound to happen. Google has outgrown this dream of feeling small while becoming massive, but the company maintains a distinctive culture, nonetheless.

Even though the culture has changed, Silverstein added, "the basic principles that underlie Google both in terms of the products and how we run internally as a company have not really changed since it started."[2] Silverstein says the company still believes work should be fun and that it remains a technology-focused and -driven company.

Larry Page believes that as long as Google organizes itself into natural or "right-sized" working groups, the company's spirit and culture will hold.

Sergey, on the other hand, says, "I actually don't think keeping the culture is a goal. I think improving the culture is. We shouldn't be like, looking back to our golden years and say, 'Oh, I wish it was the same.'"[3]

NEW MANAGEMENT STYLE

Their venture capitalists closely watched the young business enterprise's development and pressed the founders to add another member to top management, but Sergey and Larry took their time recruiting a chief executive officer. Eventually they found one who suited them. At first, they didn't give him the chief executive's title, but in time, Eric Schmidt took on the CEO position, with the Google boys serving as co-presidents. Schmidt handles almost all the key reports. Larry and Sergey are then free to pursue the creative side of the business.

This doesn't mean, however, that Brin and Page were willing to relinquish control. It is understood at Google that the founders have the final say on all major decisions. Apparently, getting the weigh-in gets more difficult as the presidents become increasingly busy.

Larry explained how the triumvirate that runs Google works:

> *Eric has the legal responsibilities of the CEO and focuses on management of our vice presidents and the sales organization. Sergey focuses on engineering and business deals. I focus on engineering and product management. All three of us devote considerable time to overall management of the company and other fluctuating needs.*[4]

~

"The goal of the company is not to monetize everything. Our goal is to change the world. Monetization is a technology to pay for it,"[5] says Eric Schmidt. And yet, two words heard repeatedly around Google are *scale* and *monetize*. These words speak to the questions, Can a service or technology be grown big enough to make it worth the effort, and can it be made profitable?

~

Google has faced the same problems that other fast-growing startups have encountered. Among them are how to manage growth without losing your soul; how to keep ideas fresh; and how to keep bright employees and avoid hiring mediocre people.

David Friedberg, a founding member of Google's corporate development team, explained that good hiring is key to Google's success. "There are certain kinds of people where it's not about the money. And Google hires those kinds of people." Friedberg left Google to start his own Internet company, WeatherBill.[6]

After the company was a few years old, Sergey and Larry realized their management structure had become too complex. By autumn 2001, the company felt top-heavy and unwieldy. They called their engineering managers to a meeting and told them they were out of jobs. Most got hired in other departments. The company was reorganized into small teams that attacked hundreds of projects all at once.

~

The founders give the employees great latitude, and they take the same latitude for themselves. Sometimes they show up unexpectedly for the wrong meeting. Sometimes they disappear entirely—zooming away in the corporate jet or taking a break to go kite surfing.[7]

Although there are meetings going on all over Google campuses all the time, Terry Winograd, Larry's academic advisor at Stanford, says, "Larry and Sergey believe that if you try to get everybody on board it will prevent things from happening. If you just do it, others will come around to realize they were attached to old ways that were not as good—no one has proven them wrong—yet."[8]

Eric Schmidt says that Google merely *appears* to be disorganized. "We say we run the company chaotically. We run it at the edge."[9]

~

Eric Schmidt says that curiosity and probing play a large part in Google's management style.

Among the frequently asked management questions are:

- How do we make the products we have the most useful?
- What is the best long-term path for the company?
- What are the next big breakthroughs in research?
- How is the competition affecting our business?

"Out of the conversation comes innovation," Schmidt notes. "Innovation is not something that I just wake up one day and say 'I want to innovate.' I think you get a better innovative culture if you ask it as a question."[10]

~

Despite Larry and Sergey's quick, smart personalities and their rollerblading approach to business, David Friedberg said they never forgot that they were running a company. "At the end of the day, it is a company and there are products, and you have to deliver the products."[11]

TEN THINGS GOOGLE HAS FOUND TO BE TRUE

When a company grows as madly as Google has, it is useful to have simple but grand guiding principles to keep everyone moving in the same direction. Employees find that these 10 principles, displayed on Google's website (under Corporate Information), help them make decisions and products that truly are Googly.

1. **Focus on the user and all else will follow.** The company strives to put the user ahead of shareholders when making corporate decisions. Additionally, Google makes these promises:
   - The website interface will be clear and simple.
   - Pages will load instantly.
   - Placement or ranking in search results is never sold to anyone.
   - Advertising must be relevant to the search and not be distracting.

2. **It's best to do one thing really, really well.** "Google does search," the company used to say. As Google grows and launches new products, it drifts farther and farther away from this maxim. Still, the company claims that other products such as Gmail, Google Desktop, and Google Maps are just part of Google's effort to improve search.

3. **Fast is better than slow.** "Google believes in instant gratification," it says, adding that "Google may be the only company in the world whose stated goal is to have users leave its website as quickly as possible."

4. **Democracy on the Web works.** "Google works because it relies on the millions of individual posting websites to determine which other sites offer content of value," explains Google on its website. This has also been referred to as "the wisdom of crowds."

5. **You don't need to be at your desk to need an answer.** This is why Google branches into technology to make search available on PDAs, on mobile phones, and in automobiles.

6. **You can make money without doing evil.** This is the most difficult and controversial of Google's precepts. For an exploration of the idea, go to the section "Don't Do Evil" in the chapter "The Vision."

7. **There's always more information out there.**
   Google has indexed more Web pages than
   any other search service, and it continually adds
   more searchable material. This is not only desirable, it is necessary as the World Wide Web
   expands.

8. **The need for information crosses all borders.**
   More than half of Google search results are sent to
   users outside the United States. Search results are
   available in approximately 118 languages, and
   Google's translation services improve continually.

9. **You can be serious without a suit.** Nothing proves
   that more than Sergey's and Larry's attire. Most
   often they are seen in Levi's and t-shirts, sometimes wearing Croc sandals. Even the head of their
   Paris office, working from a classy address near
   the opera, wears Levi's to work. Recently the
   Google boys have been known to throw sports
   jackets over their t-shirts.

10. **Great just isn't good enough.** Google tells its
    employees, "Always deliver more than expected."
    Google does not accept being the best as an end-
    point, but a starting point.

(*Note:* The Ten True Things are Google's. The expla-
nations are adapted from Google's website and other
sources.)

RIDING THE LONG TAIL

"Our business model is the long tail," said one Google employee. "Management talks about it all the time."[12]

Long-tail marketing, which was first practiced by Sears, Roebuck & Company with its big wish-book catalogs, has been developed to a double-bang level by Internet marketing companies—Google in particular. The *long-tail model* gets its name from statistical curves, such as the familiar bell curve or the Pareto curve. The curve starts at zero and rises to a peak, then drops and flattens. But it almost never returns to zero. The tail end of the curve may level out and go on seemingly forever.

In sales or marketing graphs, the top of the curve typically describes a company that has high sales, but usually with a limited number of top-selling products. Long-tail Internet companies, which can sell from huge inventories because they're not actually warehousing the goods, may indeed make money from selling the most popular products, but they also have the capacity to extract endless sales from more specialized, obscure, even weird products. In his book, *The Long Tail: Why the Future of Business Is Selling Less of More*, Chris Anderson calls this "markets without end."[13]

Eric Schmidt explained at the company's first annual meeting in 2004 that Google's advertising program was so lucrative because it captures the high end of the curve, by serving the few large advertisers, and then follows the tail by serving the millions of small advertisers all the way down to a one-person operation:

> *The surprising thing about the long tail is how long the tail is, and how many businesses (at the far end of the tail) haven't been served by traditional advertising sales. The recognition that businesses such as ours show a Pareto distribution appears to be a much deeper insight that anyone realized.*

Once Google management understood how much of the curve (especially the middle) could be tapped and maximized, it found an amazing number of ways to play the long-tail game.

20 PERCENT PROJECTS

"We encourage our employees, in addition to their regular projects, to spend 20 percent of their time working on what they think will most benefit Google," says Larry Page. "This empowers them to be more creative and innovative. Many of our significant advances have happened in this manner. For example, AdSense for Content and Google News were both prototyped in '20 percent time.' Most risky projects fizzle, often teaching us something. Others succeed and become attractive businesses."[14]

The much-applauded free-time projects give employees a sense of autonomy—one way of keeping smart people committed as the company grows more bureaucratic. "As companies grow larger, it's more difficult to allow people to be creative," acknowledged Craig Neville-Manning, Google's engineering director.[15]

Sadly, as the world business went into a decline and Google prepared itself to weather the economic storm, there were indications that the 20 percent times might be curtailed. Schmidt said that engineers may not get a lot of time and a lot of people to work on dream projects. "When the cycle comes back," he said, "we will be able to fund his brilliant vision."[16]

~

In the autumn of 2008, Google executives and a number of state and local politicos gathered at Grand Central Terminal to admire a demonstration of one of Google's most popular 20 percent projects—Google maps for the public transit system.

Google was allowed to install ten demonstration kiosks in the train station showing the best ways to get around New York City's sprawling 5,000-square-mile subway, bus, and train network.

The public transit mapping system was first introduced in 2006, and Los Angeles, California and Austin, Texas were soon added to the cities where it was available. The greater challenge comes as the more complex urban areas such as London, Tokyo, and Paris are mapped.

The project was the brainchild of California-based Avichal Garg and Chris Harrelson. When New York transit offered Google the information needed to create the maps, Garg and Harrelson weren't prepared for the sheer volume of material they would receive. They weren't sure they should continue with it. Marissa Mayer, Google's vice president for search products and user experience, told them, "Just take the data."[17] The project got done with cooperation from employees in Europe and Japan.

PERPETUAL BETA

It's not exactly a motto, but it's a phrase frequently heard in Google circles: "Launch early, iterate often."

Google sometimes is chided for releasing most of its products in beta, or during development, and keeping them there for a long time. On the minus side, this makes it seem that Google engineers can't perfect a product; they rely on the users to do that for them. It also serves as a useful excuse if a product is flawed. It's still in beta, after all.

On the plus side, users tend to do a good job at perfecting products, and Google can use the policy to maintain a high level of innovation.

"The idea that you're continually improving the product, that you're continually advancing it, I think is critical to the world of technology, and the kind of consumer technology that Google does," said Paul Buchheit, the lead engineer who developed Gmail for Google before founding his own startup, FriendFeed.

> *If they just stand still, they're going to very quickly lose their position . . . but beyond that, there's the risk that as an institution you can forget how to innovate, which can be deadly, because new competitors can come along and you won't be able to catch up with them because you've forgotten how to innovate. It's crucial that a company maintains a continual culture of innovation.*[18]

FABLED WORKPLACE

Fortune is just one of several publications to have rated Google number one on its list of best places to work.

Google has become the world's employer of choice, the mark of a new and desired work environment, and the ideal against which other companies are measured. And why not? Despite the liberal sharing of profits and a slowdown in the world economy, Google continues to do interesting work and make money.

Depending on the office location, the company provides laundry equipment for all those blue jeans and t-shirts. Employees can get haircuts, have the oil changed in their cars, and get workouts within a quick walk from their desks. There are massages, volleyball courts, swimming pools, and food—lots of food. Google even has its own cricket club at its office in Hyderabad, India.

Dressing casually is almost a requirement at Google. Most workers, including those in France and Ireland, wear blue jeans to work. Despite the casual atmosphere, Eric Schmidt says that the rule is, workers must at least wear something. The style is best described as "disheveled student."[19]

Google takes pride in its Employee Resource Groups (ERGs) such as Google Women Engineers, Black Google Network, and even Gayglers. Gayglers include the company's GLBT (gay, lesbian, bisexual, and transsexual) employees. "Google's ERGs," writes the company on its website, "create networks within the company that reach across functional and national boundaries to strengthen the company's retention programs. They provide valuable feedback about the workings of Google's HR programs and policies, as well as provide valuable opportunities for personal growth and professional development."

Then there are the stock options. These lucrative perks present a dilemma in that they both keep employees at the company and eventually allow them to fly away and either live free or start their own businesses.

One employee said he appreciates all of the perks, but what he enjoys most is working with the best and brightest people in his field in a collegial, cooperative atmosphere. Stanford Ph.D.s are so common, he said, that those who have earned them don't get much in bragging rights. "I trained as a business analyst," he explained. "When I joined Google my computer skills weren't on a plane with the engineers. But they were great in helping me learn what I needed to know."

The Google workplace of today is shaped by many factors—the expectations of Larry and Sergey's generation, the company's location in Silicon Valley, and an academic-rich environment. Even the personal histories of the founders carry weight. Larry Page places enormous importance on being a good employer.

"My grandfather," explained Page, "worked in the auto plants in Flint, Michigan. He was an assembly-line worker. During the sit-down strikes he used to carry this long iron pipe with a big chunk of lead on the end when he walked to work."[20] He did it, Page said, to protect himself from the company. "I still have the hammer. That's two generations ago, and we've come a long way. I don't think any of our employees have to carry such weapons to work."[21]

Many, including Page himself, contend that Google has much to gain from treating its workers well. "It's common sense," says Larry. "Happy people are more productive."[22]

Google didn't invent the casual workplace. It has been a Silicon Valley tradition for many decades, but the company brought the concept to new levels. The Google guys have tried to keep the Google work environment much like a college campus, only with better services. Since the software and Internet companies are constantly competing for talent, whatever Google does, other companies are motivated to do as well.

Not all of the perks are permanent, though. Google once offered a $5,000 subsidy for those who bought a hybrid car. While Google wanted to encourage clean technologies, it was never the company's intent to keep the subsidy forever.[23] As the economic downturn of 2008 hit, even Google tightened its belt.

AN ALTERNATIVE POINT OF VIEW

After *Fortune* named Google as the "Number One Best Place to Work" in 2008, a former employee who called herself "Lisa" said this about working for Google:

> *Google should not be on this list. I see you guys put performance of the company before anything else.*
>
> *The perks are just a smoke screen. Seriously. I used to work there and it was like propaganda . . . they used*

to tell us to spread the word constantly to our friends, etc. about the free food, massages! etc.

First, if you want to do well at the company you can't take a long lunch. Taking more than half an hour is looked down upon. And you just end up eating at your desk. It's there, but not really there. As for massages, there's a six-month wait list to even schedule one and by the time it rolls around there's a 90 percent chance that you won't be able to make it because of a scheduled meeting, etc.

Lastly, the managers are horrendous. There is no internal system of reviewing them. I've heard horror stories.[24]

Another employee, who wished to remain anonymous, did not echo Lisa's complaint. He felt that his work was exciting and important and that management was accessible. However, he was more than an hour late for a dinner meeting with the author because even at 6:30 P.M. he couldn't get out of Googleplex. He is the first to admit that working long hours is the norm for him.

A Google spokesman offered this insight: "It is a workplace, after all."

GOOGLEPLEX

On a sunny day in September, one of the Google development teams walked out of Googleplex, the company headquarters, and crossed the grassy campus to embark on a team-building trek along the San Francisco inner bay. As they headed out to the nature preserve, they spotted a meeting in progress on a conference bicycle, a circular contraption that allows multiple riders to pedal and talk while the front rider steers. They skirted the buses that lined surrounding streets, waiting to shuttle thousands of employees back and forth to work from homes within 50 miles of headquarters. They took note of a Google picnic setting up in an adjacent park, marked by huge balloon rainbows in Google colors. They were passed by Googlers on bikes heading to other buildings on the sprawling campus.

Google and its culture has taken over the town, especially the eastern edge of homey little Mountain View. Google now occupies 30 buildings there with an excess of three million square feet of office space. This is more than a third of Mountain View's available office space, and though growth at Google has plateaued, the company has contingent plans for even more square footage if needed. Because many of Google's buildings, including its headquarters, are on land leased from the city, they are welcome tenants. In 2007, Mountain View received about $3.8 million in revenue from Google leases.[25]

If Larry and Sergey are the twin King Arthurs of the tech world, Googleplex is its Camelot. It serves as a modern royal court. Googleplex is loaded with amenities that appeal to young or young-in-brain Googlers. There is a sand volleyball court and crazy outdoor art. Google even has its own lifeguards. Mountain View ordinances require them for the two swim-against-the-current pools.

Employees can get full-time medical care and free physicals, and there are designated private spaces for nursing mothers. The company once offered low-cost child care, but the price went up on that. Or how about a nap on one of the strategically placed nap pads? Workers can bring their dogs, as long as the mutts behave. If it seems as though Googlers don't have time to work, check out the McDonald's-style pit filled with multicolored plastic balls. It's there for holding meetings.

Most of all, Googleplex is known for its free and fabulous food. There are snack racks everywhere, three gourmet meals a day, and home food delivery for new parents.[26] It is estimated that Google was spending as much as $72 million a year feeding employees, a tab of approximately $7,530 per Googler.[27]

It became a major crisis when its original executive chef, Charlie Ayers, left to start his own restaurant. Google spent three months trying to find a replacement for Charlie, who once (occasionally) cooked for the Grateful Dead. Google food is imaginative, to say the least, and everyone wanted it to stay that way. One chef trying out for Ayers' job served sugar-pie pumpkin lasagna and cedar spring lamb chops.

Even without all the pampering, freebies, and toys, Google headquarters, in futuristic buildings that once housed Silicon Graphics, is a pleasant place to work. A vegetable garden grows in the central quad, with the output used in the cafeterias.

Larry, a devoted gadgeteer, once rode a Segway personal transporter around the campus. Segways were first replaced by electric scooters and then by bicycles. Needless to say, the bicycles are cheaper and more environmentally sound, and they became especially important as workers fought the "Google 10 (or 20)" pounds they gained eating in the cafeterias.

It is easy to find the cafeteria, the lava lamps, and the lapdogs at Google's Mountain View headquarters, but it's not as easy to find the subtly hidden-away offices of Sergey and Larry.

The office long shared by Larry and Sergey, with Eric Schmidt nearby, is tucked into a corner of Building Number 43. Their spacious work home is predictably decked out with snazzy technology. Rows of flat-screen monitors line the walls with electronic calendars, e-mail, financial information, and the Google search engine. The founders have medicine balls for ergonomics and massage chairs for relaxation, plus windows on the bustling world of Google below them and outside.

GOOGLE IN IRELAND

Not all Google facilities are as glamorous and free-wheeling as Googleplex. The Santa Monica facility is a standard Southern California office building, although Google-striped umbrellas flutter gaily on a rooftop patio, and the office is alluringly near the beach and famed Santa Monica Pier.

Perhaps the Dublin, Ireland, office best epitomizes what the Google culture has become in the world.

Google's twin towers rise above a small street in Dublin's formerly derelict Dockside area. Just a few years ago, the neighborhood was nothing but a few scattered small businesses surrounded by decaying warehouses. The area came to life after the Irish economy exploded. With the advent of the Celtic Tiger, new businesses went looking for bigger, more modern digs than were available in other parts of the lovely Georgian city.

Most Google facilities can be identified by the telltale striped umbrellas. The Dublin office is a notable exception. The Irish weather discourages outdoor eating spaces. On many days, Googlers huddle in doorways and building overhangs, smoking out of the drizzle. Here, as in California, the workforce is young, intense, and invariably dressed in Levi's and t-shirts or sweaters.

Lured by a young and international workforce, not to mention generous tax breaks, Google opened its Dublin office in 2004 with 150 people. It now is Google's largest facility aside from the headquarters in Mountain View. A sophisticated glass-and-steel building in the middle of a historic city, the European headquarters is now home to 1,350 employees. Dozens of languages are spoken at the tech center, and colorful flags of many countries hang from the ceilings.

Never mind the paucity of sunny outdoor dining areas and colorful umbrellas; Google Ireland still displays the requisite lava lamps, exercise balls, and a huge screen in the lobby that shows search activity as it occurs around the globe.

Google, like other U.S. companies such as Facebook and Dell, was drawn to Ireland because it offers a very low corporate tax of 12.5 percent. Even so, other levies, such as the tax for having a television set, can be quite high. The restaurant food tax in Dublin, for example is around 13 percent, while the tax on alcoholic drinks is about 21 percent.

Despite the weather and the consumption taxes, Google continues to expand in Dublin and its environs. Even during the Irish recession that began in 2007, Google added employees there.

TOP TEN REASONS TO WORK AT GOOGLE

While some former employees and company critics claim that Google overpromotes its glossy workplace and stimulating atmosphere, it is refreshing to have a company that at least thinks so much about the quality of work life and makes a voluntary effort to value employees and treat them with respect. This is Google's own list of employee benefits:

1. **Lend a helping hand.** With millions of visitors every month, Google has become an essential part of everyday life—like a good friend—connecting people with the information they need to live great lives.
2. **Life is beautiful.** Being a part of something that matters and working on products in which you can believe is remarkably fulfilling.
3. **Appreciation is the best motivation**, so we've created a fun and inspiring workspace you'll be glad to be a part of, including on-site doctor and dentist; massage and yoga; professional development opportunities; shoreline running trails; and plenty of snacks to get you through the day.
4. **Work and play are not mutually exclusive.** It is possible to code and pass the puck at the same time.
5. **We love our employees, and we want them to know it.** Google offers a variety of benefits, including a choice of medical programs, company-matched 401(k), stock options, maternity and paternity leave, and much more.
6. **Innovation is our bloodline.** Even the best technology can be improved. We see endless opportunity

to create even more relevant, more useful, and faster products for our users. Google is the technology leader in organizing the world's information.

7. **Good company everywhere you look.** Googlers range from former neurosurgeons, CEOs, and U.S. puzzle champions to alligator wrestlers and former Marines. No matter what their backgrounds Googlers make for interesting cube mates.

8. **Uniting the world, one user at a time.** People in every country and every language use our products. As such we think, act, and work globally—just our little contribution to making the world a better place.

9. **Boldly go where no one has gone before.** There are hundreds of challenges yet to solve. Your creative ideas matter here and are worth exploring. You'll have the opportunity to develop innovative new products that millions of people will find useful.

10. **There is such a thing as a free lunch after all.** In fact, we have them every day: healthy, yummy, and made with love.

THE BATTLE FOR BRAINPOWER

Kai-Fu Lee, a Chinese-born computer scientist, got caught in Google/Microsoft crossfire as the two companies battled for his services. Lee was Microsoft's vice president of interactive services when, in 2005, he was lured away to establish Google China. Microsoft sued Google, saying that Lee was in violation of a one-year noncompete-clause agreement he had signed with Microsoft. The courts allowed Lee to go to work for Google but prevented him from participating in projects that overlapped with Microsoft's until the case was settled. Microsoft and Google settled out of court, and Lee stayed with Google in China.

According to the Zdnet website, Lee wrote a letter in Chinese explaining that "Microsoft is an outstanding company, and there are many things we can learn from it. But Google is a company that makes me feel a shock. The reason Google gives me a shock is the passion for creating a new generation of technology. I found treasures in Google everywhere. The technology and products are way beyond just the search."

At the end of the letter, Lee gave his formula for why Google was his choice:

> *youth + freedom + transparency + new model + the general public's benefit + belief in trust = The Miracle of Google*[28]

~

The Internet and all of its trillions of websites, including Google, represent intellectual capital. The tangible assets of companies like Google are negligible compared to their precious inventories of brains and imagination.

Larry and Sergey's esteem for lofty academic achievement was present early on. When they added members to the board of directors in 2004, Larry proudly announced their credentials:

> *John Hennessy is the President of Stanford and has a Doctoral degree in computer science. Art Levinson is CEO of Genentech and has a Ph.D. in biochemistry. Paul Otellini is President and COO of Intel. We could not be more excited about the caliber and experience of these directors.*[29]

~

When Google was in its infancy, the best search engine around was AltaVista. However, its owner at the time, Hewlett-Packard, didn't seem to appreciate the talent they had on board. Google ended up hiring many AltaVista engineers, who made enormous contributions to Google's success.

One of Google's quiet strategies has been to learn from earlier Internet failures, especially Netscape. Both Eric Schmidt and Omid Kordestani came to Google from that company, which experienced a wild ride both up and down. "Google, being a generation later, was able to learn from what Netscape did well and build on it," explained Kordestani. "The best déjà vu is working with the distinguished Netscape alumni at Google."[30]

~

In a 2005 coup, Google hired World Wide Web pioneer Vint Cerf as vice president and its resident "Internet evangelist." Cerf, formerly with DARPA (Defense Advanced Research Project Agency), often is cited as the "father of the Internet." At Google he serves as something of a futurist, thinking about, anticipating, and predicting the effects of the World Wide Web on society.

~

Chris Lavoie, a Canadian who expected to become a university professor but now works at Googleplex, said it was mental stimulation that drew him to Google. Lavoie explained, "I thought university was where the hardest problems were studied, but everything is bigger here and the problems are harder to solve. The scale of the Web and the systems fascinate me. I realized this was where the biggest things were happening."[51] Lavoie gets the same reaction whenever he says he works at Google. "Jealousy. Universal jealousy."[32]

Since its founding, Google has received more than five million job applications from those wishing to work there. Google has dreamed up novel ways to find people it considers clever enough to fill their jobs. Google once erected a signboard on Route 101, the congested corridor between San Francisco and Silicon Valley, without a logo, website, or obvious message. It simply read: "{first 10-digit prime found in consecutive digits of e}.com."

Those clever enough to solve the equation came up with 7427466391.com. When they typed that number into their browser they were led to a page that presented another, more difficult problem. Those with the correct answer got a shot at a Google job interview.

The company also ran its "Google Labs Aptitude Test" as advertisements in nerdy tech publications such as the *Linux Journal.* The test included 21 complex math equations and insider-knowledge questions such as "What is the most beautiful math equation ever derived?"[33]

~

Google often acknowledges:

> *Employees may be more likely to leave us after their initial options grant fully vests, especially if the shares underlying the options have significantly appreciated in value relative to the option exercise price.*

Additionally, competition for brains in the computer world is intense: ". . . we are aware that certain of our competitors have directly targeted our employees."[34]

In an effort to keep brains in-house, Google established a Founders' Award for employees who show extraordinary entrepreneurial achievement. The awards, in the form of stock grants, were worth a great deal of money. The first two Founder's Awards, worth $12 million, were awarded to two teams of a dozen or so employees each.

The inducement backfired because those who didn't get the recognition felt overlooked. "It ended up pissing way more people off," says one veteran. Google seldom grants Founders' Awards now, preferring to dole out smaller prizes, sometimes given during a personal visit from Page or Brin.[35]

All the efforts to retain knowledge workers aside, many Googlers have left the company, often because they wanted to head their own entrepreneurial effort.

Avichal Garg, a former product manager at Google and cofounder of a startup aiming at the test-preparation industry, PrepMe.com, says, "Google was just a massive explosion and sucked in all this talent." But now, "All of these people are leaving who are relatively young and ended up with a fair bit of money. They didn't walk away with $20 million, but they walked away with $2 million. And now the cost of running a new company is so low that essentially Google financed their start-up."[36]

GUARDING THE SECRETS

Google has been and remains a secretive company. Part of the firm's reluctance to engage in orgies of public relations is common sense. Mountain View, Calif. is open but also closed. The culture spawned Andy Grove's best-selling "Only the Paranoid Survive: How to Exploit the Crisis Points that Challenge Every Company." Dr. Grove popularized the importance of chaos, which obscures underlying intent. When published, Mssrs Brin and Page were revving Google's engines, and too much chatter around the Google technical secret ingredients was unnecessary.[37]

—*Stephen E. Arnold, author and technology consultant*

Larry and Sergey spelled it out when they went public:

As a smaller private company, Google kept business information closely held, and we believe this helped us against our competitors. But, as we grow larger, information becomes more widely known. As a public company, we will of course provide you with all information required by law, and we will also do our best to explain our actions. But we will not unnecessarily disclose all of our strengths, strategies and intentions.[38]

~

Google is known for being elusive with reporters, even those covering local Mountain View news.[39] Because Google has such a large presence in its town and because Google is a publicly held company, the local newspaper feels that citizens have a right to know at least something about what's going on there. The *Mountain View Voice* complained about Google's inaccessibility in a 2007 editorial:

> *For years now—at least since the company went public and ballooned to its current size—its communications with the public have fallen somewhere between spotty and non-existent.*[40]

When the newspaper contacted Google with straight-forward, noncontroversial queries, the response was not friendly. "The most common response we've received is no response at all. The second-most common response is, 'We'll get back to you'—followed by silence."[41]

The editorial continued:

> *Ultimately, the company is hurting itself with this wall of silence. As a self-proclaimed organizer of the world's information, Google's position and continued success rely on the public's trust in its motives and actions. That trust cannot thrive unless the public feels Google is an open and forthright organization. No public acts*

of philanthropy or environmental friendliness can compensate for good old-fashioned accessibility.[42]

Even after it went public, Google was notorious for not returning telephone calls from the financial community who were seeking to understand and evaluate the business model.

Google also refuses to give earnings forecasts, and much corporate information, to analysts, which ultimately is information that filters down to shareholders. Page explained in his letter to shareholders that this position is related to management's commitment to long-term planning, even if that makes for erratic earnings:

Many companies are under pressure to keep their earnings in line with analysts' forecasts. Therefore, they often accept smaller, predictable earnings rather than larger and less predictable returns. Sergey and I feel this is harmful, and we intend to steer in the opposite direction.

Stephen Arnold writes that Google's secrecy is part of its mystique: "My take on this is that Google is a company that requires close study. The public statements capture headlines, but the inner workings of Google continue to be shrouded in the joy of insider secrets that math club members enjoyed at my high school."[43]

Google
Grows Up

In less than a decade Google has gone from guerrilla startup to 800-pound gorilla. In some ways, the company is a gentle giant. . . . But that doesn't reduce the fear factor and Google knows it.[1]

—*Kevin Kelleher,* Wired

How does the Google of today compare to what it was 10 or 11 years ago? For Sergey, it is about getting more sleep:

One thing is that we have [10,000] to 20,000 people to help us. Certainly I am not pulling all-nighters all the time like we were when were in the garage, when we were only three to four people doing everything.[2]

~

Without question, Google grew up faster than any company in recent history. In adulthood, it now faces difficult and many-sided questions. Like other grown-ups, Google looks at its responsibilities, its customers, its employees, and to society as a whole. It also must continually refine and redefine itself if the company hopes to continue its leadership role in the Internet world.

Professor Joel West of San Jose State warns that Google grows more like its rival Microsoft every day:

> *Google is growing up, but it also is gradually bureaucratizing. Can it get past the bureaucracy and still be effective? This happened at Apple and Steve Jobs had to come back and break the culture. Will Google be like Microsoft, dominant for ten years, or like Toyota, dominant for 30 years? I don't have a crystal ball to tell me that.*[3]

CONFLICTS AND CONTROVERSY

Google often has blundered into trouble simply because it's operating in such a large, unfamiliar, and diverse world. Sometimes these misunderstandings are easy to resolve, such as one that came up in Southeast Asia.

When a picture of King Bhumibol Adulyandej of Thailand, blended with that of a giraffe, appeared on YouTube, Thailand blocked YouTube in that country.

Nicole Wong, Google deputy general counsel, went to Thailand to help resolve the issue. Her meeting was on a Monday morning, and she was astounded when she saw people wearing yellow shirts and blouses in the streets, subways, offices, and markets. They were everywhere.

On that day of the week, Thais wear yellow to honor the beloved, 81-year-old titular head of their nation. Wong realized immediately that YouTube had blundered into a cultural clash. The offending image was blocked in Thailand but was available on YouTube elsewhere. YouTube was restored in Thailand.

Other conflicts, such as those involving fraud, pornography, privacy, advocating violence, and human rights, are thornier.

Click Fraud

All of the search providers have been plagued with *click fraud*, the practice of manipulating the status of a website, either to make a site look more desirable or to cause trouble or run up costs for a competing website.

There's no end to the mischief. Piggybacking and conquest buys also offend advertisers and distort the usefulness of Google advertising. *Piggybacking* occurs when smaller advertisers plant brand names, slogans, or trademarked words in the text of their own search ads to lure surfers in their direction. In a *conquest buy*, the advertiser actually buys a competitor's keyword so that its own ad is listed alongside that of the most legitimate or likely user of the keyword. Keywords aren't usually exclusive. Sometimes a company will repeatedly click on a rival's search-engine advertisements to drive up its competitor's costs.

Fraudulent clicks are the most vexing problem for Google advertisers. Certain webmasters create websites tailored to lure searchers from Google and other engines onto their website to make money from AdWords or AdSense clicks. These "zombie" sites often contain nothing but a large amount of sham content. Some are *splogs* (spam blogs), which are built on high-paying keywords. Many of these websites use content from other websites, such as Wikipedia.

Another form of trickery is a Made for AdSense (MFA) website or Web page. It has little or no real content, but is filled with advertisements so that users have no choice but to click on advertisements. Such pages were once tolerated, but because of the many complaints, Google now disables such accounts.

Some advertisers claim that 25 to 30 percent of their online advertising budget is drained off by click fraud. The actual percentage would vary according to account. Google admits that click fraud is a problem and constantly works internally to avoid it; the company also says the actual level of fraud isn't as high as some advertisers claim.

Google has taken various steps to minimize or prevent invalid clicks. Some publishers that have been blocked by Google and others report receiving a life-long ban. These sites often complain that the punishment is unjustified, but Google claims it cannot disclose specific details on click fraud, since it could reveal the nature of its proprietary click-fraud monitoring system.

Google product manager Salar Kamangar says that the company is vigilant and has prosecuted click-fraud cases, but that it becomes much more difficult across international borders. Instead, Google concentrates on spotting and preventing the fraud in the first place.

"I would characterize the losses due to click fraud as small," said Kamangar.

We have a software system that filters out fraudulent clicks even before advertisers get billed for them. We are conservative with what we count, and throw out anything that looks suspicious. We also have a team of engineers and are constantly looking for ways to update the software. We also have a team of specialists investigating reports from customers that contact us and let us know they think there is a problem.[4]

Avoiding—or Not Avoiding—Pornography

In January 2006, the Justice Department requested that Google hand over search data to support the Bush administration's defense of the Child Online Protection Act

(COPA), an Internet porn law. It is often the case that societies' most serious issues are fought over smut. In this case, Google needed to prove that it would protect customer privacy. The company also said that releasing the requested information could expose trade secrets.

Google fought the request legally and won in court. An article in *Forbes* suggested that Google vigorously defended the case not so much to protect the privacy of those using its search engine, but especially to keep a lid on how much money it gathers from pornography search and advertising:

> *A public disclosure of exactly how much pornography is on the Internet and how often people look for it—the two data points that will result from fulfilling the government's subpoena—could serve to make the Internet look bad. And Google, as its leading search engine, could look the worst.*[5]

The article continues, "Google and its competitors all benefit from porn sites, which help generate search queries and page views. But Google is the only portal company that makes nearly all of its revenues from click-through advertising. Restricting porn and porn advertising—the likely aim of COPA's sponsors—could hurt Google disproportionately."[6]

∼

None of the search engines discloses how much pornography is viewed through its sites. In fact, when America Online lists its most common searches, porn references are lifted out. Pornography or sexually explicit search topics are not seen in Google's Zeitgeist reports, either. However, Nielsen/NetRatings said that porn sites attracted 38 million viewers in December 2007 alone. This is one-fourth of all Internet surfers.[7]

Web porn is big business. About 12 percent of all websites deal with pornography in some form, and worldwide revenues from the industry are estimated at more than $97 billion each year. According to Nielsen Online, about one-quarter of employees visit Internet porn sites during working hours. M. J. McMahon, publisher of *AVN Online* magazine, reports that hits are higher during office hours than at any other time of day.

The National Center for Missing and Exploited Children estimated in 2003 that 20 percent of all pornography traded over the Internet was child pornography, and that since 1997, the number of child pornography images available on the Internet had increased by 1,500 percent.

~

YouTube has been criticized for displaying videos that include child pornography and/or violent sex. So many YouTube users are posting such a large number of videos each day that it clearly is difficult for the company to police such matters. However, a spokesman noted:

> *For YouTube we have strict rules on what's allowed, and a system that enables anyone who sees inappropriate content to report it to our 24/7 review team and have it dealt with promptly. . . . Given the volume of content uploaded on our site, we think this is by far the most effective way to make sure that the tiny minority of videos that break the rules come down quickly.*[8]

~

Google itself doesn't try to keep pornography out of the search results. Searches of sexually explicit key words show plenty of sponsored links, or advertisements. And perhaps it was an accident, but Google Street View once showed prostitutes gathered on a street corner in California.

However, the portal offers a filter for those who wish to protect themselves or their children from prurient words and images. Some critics say the filter is so crude that it also eliminates websites of the White House, IBM, the American Library Association, and clothing manufacturer Liz Claiborne. Google concurs that the filter errs on the side of caution:

> *Many Google users prefer not to have adult sites included in their search results. Google's SafeSearch*

screens for sites that contain this type of information and eliminates them from search results. While no filter is 100 percent accurate, Google's filter uses advanced proprietary technology that checks keywords and phrases, URLs and Open Directory categories. When SafeSearch is turned on, sites and web pages containing pornography and explicit sexual content are blocked from search results.[9]

Those wishing to use the blocker can go to Google.com, type SafeSearch in the search box, and a popup appears allowing SafeSearch to be activated or switched off.

Nevertheless, if the filter were better, more people might use it. "If Google put some of its smart people on this task, they could do a much better job than they have so far," said Ben Edelman, a student fellow at the Harvard Law School's Berkman Center for Internet and Society. "They've got a lot of smart people. It would be shocking if their great engineers couldn't do better. The question is whether that's a priority for Google."[10]

PRIVACY ISSUE

"Privacy is dead, get over it," famously declared Sun Microsystems founder Scott McNealy.[11]

~

On one hand, Google goes to court to defend the privacy of those using its search engine. Eric Schmidt emphasizes that Google depends on the trust of its users, adding, "It would be a disaster for the company if that privacy were compromised by a privacy leak or some very bad government action that we couldn't stop under threat of tanks."[12]

On the other hand, Google frequently is accused of invading privacy through its advertising programs, its map applications, its e-mail service, and in other ways. Google's "Internet evangelist" Vint Cerf echoed McNealy's point of view in a speech he gave to the Washington Technology Alliance's annual luncheon: " . . . nothing you do ever goes away, and nothing you do ever escapes notice . . . there isn't any privacy, get over it."[13]

Ken Boehm, chairman of the National Legal and Policy Center, disagreed: "Perhaps in Google's world privacy does not exist, but in the real world individual privacy is fundamentally important and is being chipped away bit by bit every day by companies like Google. Google's hypocrisy is breathtaking."[14]

Privacy is one of the topics that scare people most about Google. "Google knows more and more about us, but right now there's almost nothing we can do to find out exactly what it does with that information," observed Frank Pasquale, an associate professor at Seton Hall University School of Law and a proponent for reining in

Google. "We want to make powerful entities on the Internet accountable."[15]

Whenever someone lands on a Google page, they get a cookie unless they already have one. In that case, Google reads and records the ID number. Using even more sophisticated *deep packet inspection* technology, Google can observe a user's entire Web browsing experience, including all URLs visited, all searches, and actual pages viewed.[16]

The company really did not want to spoil the purity of its proudly sparse home page, but due to pressure from activists, Google finally added an additional seven letters. The word? *Privacy*. By clicking on the word, Google users can check out the company's official stand on privacy issues.

ADVERTISING PRODUCTS

Tracking information is a key part of Google's advertising programs. Advertisers love the idea that Google programs allow them to verify and analyze Web traffic and information about those who click on their ads.

Gerald Reischl, author of a German book titled *The Google Trap*, is especially concerned about the information collected using Google Analytics, a free program for website owners to keep track of usage patterns on their site. The data, claims Reischl, is also saved by

Google, and transferred to the United States in violation of German law. "Analytics is Google's most dangerous opportunity to spy," says Reischl.[17]

Hendrik Speck, professor at the applied sciences university in Katserslautern, says that compared with what Google collects and knows, intelligence agencies look "like child protection services." The information, he says, could be used to target advertising many years into the future. And, he says, "The more data Google collects from its users, the higher the price it can ask for advertisements."[18]

According to Peter Fleischer, Google's Paris-based Global Privacy Counsel, Reischl's concern is unfounded. "We collect a lot of data," says Fleischer, "but nothing that identifies any particular person."[19]

The data can be used, however, to influence the behavior of Web searchers. Internet companies like Google and Yahoo! have been expanding the use of so-called "behavioral targeting" technology to tap vast amounts of accumulated data in an effort to boost advertising revenue.

Behavioral targeting comes in a number of permutations, though all serve the same purpose of examining what Internet users are visiting, buying, and looking for not only on their sites, but also elsewhere on the Web in order to construct a marketing profile for advertisers. The payoff could be considerable. The more accurately an ad is targeted, the more an advertiser is willing to pay for it.[20]

Efforts to prevent click fraud also might be seen as an invasions of privacy. AdSense publishers can choose from a number of click-tracking programs. These programs display detailed information about the visitors who click on the ads. Publishers can use this to determine whether they have been victims of click fraud.

GMAIL

"The most commonly voiced fear is Google's unique capacity to track what we're thinking based on what we're looking for," wrote *The Boston Globe*. "Google can track every name, place and topic we search. The company can learn even more about people who use Gmail, the social networking site Orkut or another of Google's popular personalized services."

Using AdSense technology, Gmail, Google's free Web-based e-mail service, delivers ads into e-mail messages linked to the topic of the e-mail itself. Google uses a totally automated system to link words to their ads, but still, if this can be done, it leaves some people with the sneaking suspicion that Gmail snooping also could be easy.

The Gmail program has been well received, despite privacy concerns. "Our competitors haven't been able to match Gmail's clean interface and huge power," says Google. We currently offer about 2.7GB of searchable storage for free. We also made it easier to sign up for Gmail by using your mobile phone, while making it hard for spammers to get accounts."[21]

STREET VIEW

Indignation over privacy has been especially strong from abroad. The British newspaper *The Independent* wrote, "One of its new ventures, Google Street View, makes government CCTV surveillance look amateur."[22]

Some people became alarmed when they realized Google Street View cameras could zoom in so closely that in one case, people could be seen inside the house. Aaron and Christine Boring, an American couple, unsuccessfully sued Google for $25,000 for showing their house on Google Street View.

"I'm convinced if you look at the actions of Google," said the Borings' attorney, Dennis Moskal, "for a company that says 'don't do evil,' it appears that they didn't have proper internal controls on the people driving around taking these pictures."[23]

In its response to the Borings' lawsuit, Google quoted from a legal text:

Complete privacy does not exist in this world except in a desert, and anyone who is not a hermit must expect

and endure the ordinary incidents of the community
life of which he is a part. It usually is not against the
law to photograph a house from the street, as long as
the photographer does not trespass on private
property.[24]

The small northern German town of Molfsee—not at all
happy at the prospect of becoming part of Street View—
anticipated the arrival of Google's fleet of dark-colored
Opel Astras with cameras on top. The photography vehicles already had shown up in other parts of Germany,
snapping photographs for Google Street View. The 5,000
citizens of Molfsee took fast action, getting the local coun-
cil to pass a road traffic act that would require Google to
get a permit for the picture-taking. Local politicians then
refused to issue the permit. Other parts of Germany were
considering enacting similar ordinances.

"These pictures, which are available for retrieval
worldwide over the Internet, could easily be linked to
satellite photos, address databanks and other personal
data," warned Germany's Federal Commissioner for
Data Protection, Peter Schaar.[25]

While Google software apparently blurs license plate
numbers and faces so as to make them unrecognizable,
and anyone who appears in a picture can request that
the picture be removed, those safeguards do not seem
to be enough for many people. Street View easily can

provide other damaging information, and, especially when combined with buildings viewed from above by satellite, could be quite useful to stalkers or anyone with criminal intent.

In Japan, a group of lawyers and professors asked Google to suspend its Street View service there. "We strongly suspect that what Google has been doing deeply violates a basic right that humans have," said Yasuhiko Tajima, a professor of constitutional law at Sophia University and head of The Campaign Against Surveillance Society. "It is necessary to warn society that an IT giant is openly violating privacy rights, which are important rights that the citizens have, through this service."[26]

~

Google CEO Eric Schmidt knows how it feels to have his private information splashed all over cyberspace. In 2004, Elinor Mills, a reporter for the tech-news website CNET, decided to discover how much personal information she could collect on the Internet about Schmidt. She Googled him and learned Schmidt's net worth ($1.5 billion), home address (somewhere in Atherton), and the names of his guests at a political fundraiser. The main guests would be Al and Tipper Gore, who danced as Elton John belted out "Bennie and the Jets." She discovered that Schmidt is an amateur pilot and, like Brin and Page, has cruised the Burning Man Festival in the Nevada desert.

Schmidt was irate, insisting the company would blacklist all CNET reporters for a year. In response to critics, Google ended the boycott after a month.[27]

"Privacy, at the end of the day," noted Eric Schmidt, "is how you feel about your privacy. People feel OK with ads about what you are doing but not about who you are. Privacy will be an evergreen issue."[28]

"What I want in the [Google] privacy policy," said Helen Nissenbaum, professor in the Department of Media, Culture, and Communication at New York University, "is something that says we will use your information x, y, and z, and we will not use it for anything else, and we will never change this policy."[29]

Privacy may not be as cold and buried as it might appear:

- Google and a coalition of other Internet companies signed an agreement to safeguard private information and freedom of speech on the Internet. For more on that pact, go to the section "Hello, Human Rights," in this chapter.
- Google's tech support and privacy pages provide instructions on how to block a website from a search engine, as well as how to get rid of cached or historical versions of the site.

- In the past few years, regulators in Europe, advocacy groups, and others effectively pressured search engines to limit the time they retain personal information. Ask.com now offers searchers the option of having their information stored for no more than a few hours. Yahoo! slashed the time it stores personal data to three months. Google has trimmed the time it retains personal information from 18 to 9 months and pared the lifespan of its cookies from 30-plus years to 2 years.[30]
- There are rumblings in the U.S. Congress to pass online privacy legislation that would give consumers the right to opt out of tracking of their Web activities.[31]
- Italian Prime Minister Silvio Berlusconi has vowed to push for an international agreement to regulate the Internet and ensure greater user privacy.[32]
- Most browsers, Google's included, now incorporate a privacy feature that covers a Web searcher's tracks on the Internet. Not to be fooled as to its most obvious purpose, most techies refer to the item as "porn mode."

CAN THEY SNOOP—AND WILL THEY TELL?

They have amassed more information about people in ten years than all the governments of the world put together. They make the Stasi and the KBG look like the innocent old granny next door. This is of immense significance. If someone evil took them over, they could easily become Big Brother.[35]

—Andrew Keen, British-born author,
Internet critic, and Silicon Valley entrepreneur

Google freely admits that it collects various sorts of information about users. However, the company says it does not collect personal identifying data such as credit-card information, phone numbers, or buying history—unless a user signs up for a service such as Checkout.

Since Google began emphasizing *cloud computing*, or individual computing done on Google's own website, its products present even more opportunities to snoop. For example, its Desktop Search indexes a client's entire desktop of files, which means they are then searchable. However, the information is stored on Google's website.

Google warns, "We may share [private] information . . . [if] we conclude that we are required by law or have a good faith belief that access, preservation or disclosure of such information is reasonably necessary to protect the rights, property or safety of Google, its users or the public."

Perhaps the most scathing comments on the privacy issue came in a 2004 *Mother Jones* article:

So the question is not whether Google will always do the right thing—it hasn't and it won't! It's whether Google, with its insatiable thirst for your personal data, has become the greatest threat to privacy ever known, a vast informational honey pot that attracts hackers, crackers, online thieves, and—perhaps most worrisome of all—a government intent on finding convenient ways to spy on its own citizenry.[34]

"How many people," asks Sergey Brin, "do you think had embarrassing information about them disclosed yesterday because of some cookie? Zero. It never happens. Yet I'm sure thousands of people had their mail stolen yesterday, or identity theft."[35]

Actually, the number of times information is compromised may be small, but it's not zero. There was a case in the Netherlands in which Google did not spy, but its applications were used to snoop. A chief technology officer installed a "backdoor" server in the company's hosting center, setting it up to forward information from a corporate director's e-mail to the so-called *spybox*, a Gmail account used as a document drop. The CTO seemed to have information that he shouldn't have had, and eventually he went too far: " . . . he forwarded private (love) mail of one of (the company's) directors to his wife. She provided these e-mails to us, which were sent from an anonymous Gmail account. Their marriage was already heading for a divorce, but the disclosed e-mails and dishonorable allegations about the victimized director created an unworkable situation."[36]

A Dutch court ordered Google to reveal the information associated with the account, and the Internet Provider (IP) address used to access it. The culprit was then
caught. The company's lawyer said it is "surprising how
easy it is to harass innocent people with anonymous
(Gmail) accounts. The verdict shows that U.S.-based
Google Inc. is willing to comply [with] Dutch law, and
that the privacy of a victim 'overrules' the privacy of the
person who did wrong. As it should be."[37]

HELLO, HUMAN RIGHTS

"There's a sub text to 'Don't be evil,' and that's 'Don't be
illegal,'" said Vint Cerf, one of the founding fathers of
the Internet. Cerf now serves as the chief Internet evangelist at Google.[38]

~

When Larry and Sergey first started on their journey
into the world of search, they were driven and excited
by the science and the possibilities that technology presented. They may not have realized what vast power
would be assigned to Google and surely didn't fully
grasp the responsibility that would attend that power.

"Google may be the first entity humankind has ever
known with the global economic power and social

influence to take the ethical high road and treat free and open expression like a moral absolute," said Jonathan Askin, a Brooklyn Law School professor and lawyer for Internet and telecommunications clients. "If Google doesn't have the wherewithal to exert its influence for the good of humanity, I don't know who will have the courage going forward."[39]

Worries over human rights and Internet usage are serious. In 2006, Yahoo! Inc. turned over e-mails and other information to the Chinese government, resulting in the imprisonment of journalist Shi Tao and writer Wang Xiaoning. Yahoo! later apologized for the action and provided financial support to the prisoners' families and asked the U.S. government to intervene.

THE GREAT CHINESE FIREWALL

In the fall of 2002, the Chinese government began blocking access to Google and a few other search engines. These engines contained various ways of finding information the Chinese authorities wanted to keep from its citizens. Within two weeks, the service was restored, because, according to some sources, Chinese citizens were outraged by the blockage. Now when Chinese searchers click on a banned link, they are directed instead to a government-approved site.

When Google reentered the China market—which is 230 million people—the company decided to abide by government censorship restrictions, despite an outcry from many that the company was giving in to a government that abused human rights.

Sergey Brin admitted that it was legitimate for Google to refuse to do business in China, given the circumstances. But, he added, there was an alternative path. Give the Chinese people at least some access to information, even though in some ways it would be limited. In addition to Google.cn, the official site, Brin noted that the Chinese people also have the option of logging on to Google.com, where the information would be uncensored but the service would be much slower. At last tally, the majority of Chinese Web surfers were choosing the slower but more informative service.

"We think we have made a reasonable decision, though we cannot be sure it will ultimately be proven to be the best one," Brin said. "We've begun a process that we hope will better serve our Chinese users."[40]

". . . When you add it all up, we think we're helping to advance the cause of change in China," said Andrew McLaughlin, Google's head of global public policy.[41]

Chinese government officials expressed their view this way: "Any trade and commercial cooperation should be carried out within the framework of laws. We hope that the relevant companies, when undertaking business operations, can abide by Chinese laws and regulations."[42]

Perhaps it was purely a business decision, but later the same year Google announced a major investment in Baidu, a leading Chinese search engine.

~

Other repressive regimes also have taken swipes at Google. For a time, Iran shut down Google blogs in that country because it did not like the discussion going on.

According to the Reporters without Borders (RSF) "Internet enemy list," the following states engage in pervasive Internet censorship: Cuba, Maldives, Myanmar/Burma, North Korea, Syria, Tunisia, Uzbekistan, and Vietnam.

PRINCIPLES OF FREEDOM

Google, along with Microsoft, Yahoo!, and other Internet companies, signed a voluntary code in 2008 spelling out "principles of freedom of expression and privacy." The principles are fairly general, but if taken literally could be quite difficult for Internet companies to adhere to. Still, the pact is a giant step in the right direction.

Microsoft explained in a company news release:

From the Americas to Europe to the Middle East to Africa and Asia, companies in the information and communications industries face increasing government pressure to comply with domestic laws and policies that require censorship and disclosure of personal information in ways that conflict with internationally recognized human rights laws and standards.[43]

A diverse coalition of organizations launched the Global Network Initiative, which establishes guidelines for resisting government efforts to enlist companies in acts of censorship and surveillance. The group is collaborating with other companies, investors, civil society organizations, and academics to establish and implement Principles on Freedom of Expression and Privacy, a doctrine based on internationally recognized laws and standards for human rights.

Mike Posner, president of Human Rights First, said,

In today's world, it is urgent for Internet providers and other communications companies to challenge government censorship and intrusion into personal privacy. These practices often lead to tragic consequences for front line human rights activists. Through this initiative, we take a crucial first step in advancing free expression and privacy, at a time when government interference with these basic human rights is on the rise. . . . Technology must no longer be used to trample basic human rights.[44]

COPYRIGHT INFRINGEMENT

In an open letter to the 8,000 members of the Authors Guild, President Roy Blount Jr. wrote:

> *The Guild had sued Google in September 2005, after Google struck deals with major university libraries to scan and copy millions of books in their collections. Many of these books were older books in the public domain, but millions of others were still under copyright protection. Nick Taylor, the president of the Guild, saw Google's scanning as "a plain and brazen violation of copyright law." Google countered that digitizing these books represented a "fair use" of the material. Our position was: The hell you say. Of such disagreements, lawsuits are made.*[45]

This was the reaction to Google's grandiose scheme to scan all the books it could and make them available on the Internet. Google described the project as a great gift to humanity. One Google employee told the *New Yorker's* Jeffrey Tobin, "I think of Google Books as our moon shot."[46] Authors and publishers saw it differently.

THE AUTHORS' REVOLT

Indeed, the Authors Guild filed suit, as did the Association of American Publishers and several major publishing houses. Later, the European Parliament began scrutinizing the company for potential copyright infringement.

The president of Bibliotheque Nationale de France, Jean-Noel Jeanneney, called the project "a piece of Anglo-Saxon cultural imperialism."[47]

Two years after the suits were filed, Google and the plaintiffs reached a U.S. settlement that has the potential of revolutionizing the publishing industry and the way people access books. It also set up a powerful moneymaker for Google.

First, let's take a look at what the dispute was all about.

Grand Ambitions

Larry Page took a personal interest in assembling a massive library of books on Google's website. He made a visit to his alma mater, the University of Michigan, in mid-2004, and soon afterward Google quietly started digitizing books from UM's library. Later in the year, the Google Print for Libraries project was made public. The initiative has had several name changes and lately is called the Print Library Project.

"Call me weird," said Sergey Brin, "but I think there are a lot of advantages to reading books online. You don't have to look at it at a funny angle, and today's monitors have better resolution than ever."[48]

Eventually, 30 libraries, including Oxford, Stanford, and Harvard universities and the New York Public Library, joined with Google in digitizing books. Google pays the library for the right to copy the book by providing the library itself with a digital copy. Within four years, Google had digitized more than seven million volumes.

Google promoted the book project as a public service, as a way to make knowledge more readily available and help authors get exposure for their ideas and for their writing. Unfortunately, there seemed to be little or no mechanism to benefit those who created the work.

Google had a legal right to copy about one-sixth of all books, the ones old enough to have never been copyrighted and those that have outlived their copyright protection. About 85 percent of all books are still under copyright. Many of those are out of print, but they remain the intellectual property of those who wrote them. About 10 percent of all books are both in print and copyrighted.

After the lawsuits were filed, Google scaled back its dreams and began to operate this way: "When you click on a search result for a book from the Library Project, you'll see basic bibliographic information about the book, and in many cases, a few snippets—a few sentences showing your search term in context. If the book is out of copyright, you'll be able to view and download the entire book. In all cases, you'll see links directing you to online bookstores where you can buy the book and libraries where you can borrow it."[49]

Only certain books, those that Google could use for free, would be available for downloading in their entirety; others could be purchased, by linking to booksellers. Google's book search project began to look like a big, online bookstore.

The Snippet Defense

Google continued the scanning and stood up for its right to digitize all books. The lawsuits argued that Google's two claims—that it was merely using a snippet allowed under fair use rules and that the digitization could spur book sales—were insufficient: Even if Google did use only snippets, the Authors Guild claimed that the company had no right to scan the copyrighted books in the first place. Digital copying is one of the uses covered under copyright law. Google's "snippet" argument raised another question among authors—if the search engine would show only tiny excerpts, why would Google bother to scan and store the entire book? This implied that Google had something else in mind. Certainly the books online represented a chance to sell a lot of ads.

"Google is doing something that is likely to be very profitable for them," said Paul Aikin of the Authors Guild, "and they should pay for it. It's not enough to say that it will help the sales of some books. If you make a movie of a book, that may spurt sales, but that doesn't mean you don't license the books."[50]

Other Internet services have ideas similar to Google's. Microsoft spent $2.5 million to scan 100,000 books, but is no longer sponsoring the work. Amazon also has scanned hundreds of thousands of books for the e-book service, Kindle. Both companies took different approaches, ones that dealt writers and publishers into the game.

Whose Property Is It, Anyway?

The attitude of Google's management did not endear it to authors and publishers. Schmidt declared that copyright is not an "absolute" right, and that Google is willing to push the envelope on this issue. "That's probably correct," he said. "If there's a legal case, we're going to favor the legal one that favors the users."[51]

Sergey Brin surely wasn't surprised at the uproar over copyright infringement. As a graduate student, he worked not only on Stanford's book digitization project, but also on a venture involving automated detection of copyright violations.

Additionally, the company founders clearly understood the value of intellectual output when it is their own. In its prospectus for its initial public offering, Google declared, "Our intellectual property rights are valuable, and any inability to protect them could reduce the value of our products, services and brand."

All About Advertising

The U.S. Congress conducted a legal review of the book project and published its own report. "The Library

Project has the potential to be a great boon to scholarship research, and the public in general. It is, nevertheless, commercial in nature because Google anticipates that it will enhance its service's utilization by the public and concomitantly increase advertising fees."[52]

The Congressional report went on to say that creating an index of books alone, and including a snippet of the text, most likely would not be a copyright infringement. However, the report agreed that the conflict arises when Google copies the entire book, whether it makes the whole book available to searchers or not. Digitizing is a transformation of the original work, and the digital version could very well belong to Google, not to the author, publisher, or the world in general.

THE GAME-CHANGING SETTLEMENT

After two years of negotiations, Google and the plaintiffs reached a resolution that seemed to satisfy writers and publishers and to serve Google's clients. The deal makes electronic books available to public libraries that they never could have afforded otherwise. Additionally, readers and researchers will have greater access to rare and out-of-print books.

First of all, the $125 million settlement included $45 million in payments to authors whose books Google already had scanned without their permission. Google would pay

crossroads of new technologies and existing laws to provide those answers, helping Google build innovative and important products for our users around the world.[56]

    —Recruiting advertisement for lawyers to work at Google

"We *joust* at the crossroads . . . " might be a more appropriate wording of this Google advertisement for lawyers. From patent, copyright, and trademark infringement to click fraud to wrongful dismissal, Google spends a lot of time in court. While it is true that Google makes a large target, it also is true, as the company itself notes, that it is operating in a field littered with uncertainties begging to be resolved in the courts of law. Some of the lawsuits address key issues that could define both Google and the Internet of the future.

In terms of Google's viability as a company, the most important of all the lawsuits pitted Google against its business partner, Yahoo!. It started in May 1999, when GoTo .com filed a patent application called "System and method for influencing a position on a search result list generated by a computer network search engine." The request was granted in July 2001, as U.S. patent 6269361. A related patent also was awarded in Australia. It seems the GoTo .com patent became the format for Google's AdWords.

Just a year later, Overture—prior to its acquisition by Yahoo!—initiated copyright infringement proceedings under this patent against Google, claiming that AdWords technology borrowed too much from Overture. In February 2002, Google had introduced AdWords Select, which allowed marketers to bid for higher placement in market sections—a tactic that had similarities to Overture's search-listing auctions.

Following Yahoo!'s acquisition of Overture, the lawsuit was settled, with Google agreeing to issue 2.7 million shares of common stock to Yahoo! in exchange for a perpetual license for Overture.

Companies large and small have sued Google multiple times over trademark infringement. They include Geico, American Blind & Wallpaper, and American Airlines. In 2004, Google started allowing advertisers to bid on a wide variety of search terms in the United States and Canada, including the trademarks of their competitors. In May 2008, this policy was expanded to the United Kingdom and to Ireland. Google advertisers are restricted from using other companies' trademarks in their advertising text if the trademark has been registered with Google's Advertising Legal Support team.

~

Unfortunately, Google often settles its suits out of court, with the details of the settlement kept secret. When this happens, important legal questions remain unanswered and murky legal waters remain turgid. Such was the case with American Airlines. The airline was offended that when Google searchers entered AA.com, its website, the results included websites unrelated to, or in competition with, the airline.

American Airlines asked Google to stop selling its trademarked terms to other advertisers. Google, it said, was "utilizing our brand that we've built for more than 60 years for the benefit of someone else."[57]

The American Airlines suit was settled out of court, and the details were confidential. It wasn't clear what the suing companies gained and what Google learned. However, if the name "American Airlines" or AA.com now is entered into the Google search box, only references to American appear.

Google has good reason to work with advertisers to settle this sort of dispute. John Gustafson, director of distribution and Internet strategy at the former Northwest Airlines explained, "If Google has an inability to help us resolve issues about abuses of our brand that would impact our decision to participate in future forms of advertising."[58]

～

Some legal battles, such as the one with Viacom, have been long and hard-fought. Viacom brought legal action against Google and YouTube for $1 billion, claiming that

YouTube airs its content without paying for it. Comedians Jon Stewart and Stephen Colbert were called as witnesses in the case, which revolved around YouTube clips from *The Daily Show* and *The Colbert Report*. Viacom is one of the biggest creators of television programming in the world.

Google went postal when it was ordered to turn over YouTube user data to Viacom. Google again claimed that the privacy of its users would be violated. Google denied virtually all of Viacom's infringement accusations and volleyed back one of its own: "By seeking to make carriers and hosting providers liable for Internet communications, Viacom's complaint threatens the way hundreds of millions of people legitimately exchange information, news, entertainment and political and artistic expression," Google said in answer to Viacom's suit.[59]

"Viacom is a company built from lawsuits, look at their history," said Eric Schmidt.[60]

Finally, the two companies reached an agreement allowing Google to anonymize the information before letting it go to Viacom.

Although the Viacom suit remains unresolved, *The Daily Show* began putting all its shows up for free on its own website and allowing viewers to share them.

In a move that is typical of Silicon Valley companies, even as Viacom and Google were locked in combat, they announced a joint effort to test video advertising. The joint project will allow website owners to put video clips from Viacom, including *SpongeBob SquarePants* and MTV's *Laguna Beach,* on their pages. The clips would contain advertisements from which Google, Viacom, and other producers will collect revenue.

When the Italian company Mediaset, controlled by Prime Minister Silvio Berlusconi, sued YouTube in a similar video-sharing dispute, a Google spokeswoman said her company didn't see the need for the suit. "There is no need for legal action. . . . We prohibit users from uploading infringing material and we cooperate with all copyright holders to identify and promptly remove infringing content as soon as we are officially notified."[61]

~

In 2008, Google India was ordered by the Bombay High Court to reveal the identity of a blogger known only as "Toxic Writer," who is accused of defaming Gremach Infrastructure, a small construction outfit. Google did not immediately turn over the information but may be forced to as the case moves forward.[62]

~

In 2002, Brian Reid, a 52-year-old, respected Silicon Valley engineer, was hired at Google for a senior management position. Less than two years later, Dr. Reid was fired. He sued Google for age discrimination. Reid, an experienced high-tech executive, claimed he was let go because he didn't fit into Google's youth-focused culture.

Reid claimed that he was subjected to many derogatory age-related remarks at Google. He was told he was slow, sluggish, and fuzzy, and that his ideas were "obsolete" and "too old to matter." He was referred to as the "old guy" and "old fuddy-duddy."[63]

When asked about the possibility that Brin and Page were youth-obsessed and controlling, Eric Schmidt, himself in his 50s, didn't see the issue as a problem: "The beauty of Larry and Sergey is that they are well-known quantities, that if you don't want to work with them, please don't. Slavery was made illegal years ago."[64]

GOOGLE GETS AN AIRPLANE

"No wonder the Google boys were so far out of the loop on their net neutrality lobbying effort," the Rat remarked to his minions over the top of his hard-copy of the *Wall Street Journal*. "They've been distracted by other, more important issues—like who gets what size bed on their corporate plane."[65]

It seemed like the end of an innocent but thrilling era of simplicity when in 2005 Sergey and Larry acquired an airplane. They leased (from themselves) a Boeing 767-200 wide-body jet, which typically seats 200 passengers, and had it outfitted to meet their needs. It became a party jet with two staterooms, sitting and dining areas, and a large galley with seating for 50.

Well, Bill Gates has a 767, so sharing one between Brin and Page seemed almost frugal.

The Google guys requested typically interesting modifications to their flying space, including hammocks that would hang from the ceiling. As for the beds, Eric Schmidt reportedly resolved a dispute over bed size by parental decree: "Sergey, you can have whatever bed you want in your room; Larry, you can have whatever kind of bed you want in your bedroom. Let's move on."[66]

Not only did the outfitting of the plane make headlines, so did the berthing of it. The company pays $1.3 million each year to NASA to park the plane at Moffett Field, which is a hop and a jump from Google headquarters. This is an estimated four times the cost of parking at nearby San Francisco or San Jose international airports.

Google now has several planes in the fleet, including a Dornier Alpha Jet fighter plane. Strictly speaking, the planes don't belong to Google, but rather to H211 LLC, a somewhat mysterious company reportedly controlled by Google top brass. Google will not talk about H211 LLC ownership, other than to say that Google itself holds no ownership position in the company.

As part of the Moffett Field deal, NASA gets to place instruments on the aircrafts and use some of them for atmospheric research. In one instance, the Boeing 767 carried NASA scientists and those from the SETI Institute to observe the Aurigid meteor shower. NASA, however, gets to use the plane only when Google does not. According to Web reports, NASA planned to use the jet in the summer of 2008 to observe and record data from the reentry of the Jules Verne ATV-1 space freighter. However, NASA had to find another plane (an old DC-8 as it turned out) to document the burn-up in Earth's atmosphere. Google needed its plane to shuttle guests to Montana for the wedding of San Francisco Mayor Gavin Newsom.

GOOGLE GETS A SATELLITE

Sergey Brin, Larry Page, and their wives flew to Vandenberg Air Force Base on the central California coast in the late summer of 2008 to view the launch of a satellite carrying the Google logo into space. The eye-in-the-sky was propelled into the atmosphere by Boeing on a blazing Delta2 Rocket. For two such space-crazy individuals as Larry and Sergey, it was a thrill.

GeoEye-1 has a deal with Google, giving it exclusive commercial rights to the imagery provided by the satellite. The search giant will use the data on their mapping services, Google Maps and Google Earth. The GeoEye-1 satellite is also part of the NextView program of the U.S. National Geospatial-Intelligence Agency.

Having its own space on a satellite gives Google greater control over the images it receives and uses. Google will be able to provide higher, finer images, making the views of Earth and maps more detailed and easier to use. The satellite will constantly refresh images and make them current. It will orbit 423 miles up and circle Earth more than a dozen times a day. In one day, it can collect color images of an area the size of New Mexico or a black-and-white image the size of Texas.

In spite of the improvements, Google would like to see even better pictures someday:

The new satellite is limited to releasing images for commercial use at no higher than 50 centimeters (cm) resolution by government restrictions. Most of the high resolution satellite imagery is already at 60–100 cm resolution. So, this new satellite imagery will at best be slightly higher resolution. Google Earth also has acquired higher resolution aerial imagery (e.g. taken from planes) that is as high as 5 cm resolution (see Las Vegas for example). Although details haven't been made available, it is possible the satellite is capable of higher resolution imagery. Maybe someday the government will allow higher resolution imagery to be sold.[67]

The upgrades weren't immediately seen on Google, however. "This new satellite will not mean Google Earth will suddenly have live data," wrote Google on its website.

It will still be typically several weeks to a few months before new data is put into Google Earth. In addition, the satellite is still dependent on having the right weather conditions before getting a good photo (no clouds, haze, smoke, dust, right angle of the sun) worth putting into Google Earth. But, the faster data acquisition should speed things up some. Having more satellites will definitely improve the chances for new data.[68]

— Good Citizen — Google

Google has a rich list of corporate, volunteer, and philanthropic programs designed to make the world a better place. Some of the beneficial projects reside within or come out of Google search. For example, based on the number of searches for flu and cold medicine, Google has helped identify parts of the world experiencing flu epidemics. Google maps strive to help people find their way around many cities on foot, by bicycle, or via the most environmentally friendly way possible.

Google has numerous programs specifically targeted to better education, particularly in science. These are a few of the activities:

- The Summer of Code is a three-month, \$2 million program for computer science students. Google offers student developers stipends to write code for various open-source projects. In 2008, the company partnered with 174 open-source, free software, and technology-related groups to identify and fund projects. Nearly 7,100 proposals were received, of which 1,125 were selected. While Google uses the event to look for promising recruits, the purpose is not recruiting. It is to develop a new array of open-source coding.

- In October 2006, together with LitCam and UNESCO's Institute for Lifelong Learning, Google launched the Literacy Project, offering resources for teachers, literacy groups, and anyone interested in promoting reading.

- Google gives the Anita Borg Scholarship to outstanding women studying computer science in the United States, Canada, Australia, and Europe.

- Kids visit Google regularly for hands-on workshops and to learn about exciting careers in technology.

- Google is one of the sponsors for the annual Sally Ride Science Festival, in which hundreds of girls in grades 5 through 8 and their parents spend the day at Google. They attend workshops, participate in science activities, and learn more about careers in technology. They also get a terrific lunch.

- "Introduce a Girl to Engineering" week takes place annually as part of U.S. National Engineers Week.

Employees at several Google offices bring their daughters to work for a day. Google also links up with schools and other organizations to allow other girls to take part in the day.

GOOGLE.ORG—THE PHILANTHROPIC PART

While the Black Google Network (BGN), an employee-driven resource group, was out and about helping rebuild New Orleans after Hurricane Katrina and then raising money for engineering students through the United Negro College Fund, other factions within Google were doing their own good deeds. At the same time, Google.org seemed to scan the whole earth for worthwhile projects.

Page and Brin got Google.org under way at the time they went public by pushing a plan to shareholders to commit resources, a share of profits, and employee time to attack issues they thought to be the most urgent challenges for society.

Google.org is a hybrid philanthropy through which the founders pledged to use both private and nonprofit resources for the good of the world. They go by the 1 percent rule, which means that 1 percent of Google's equity and profits, as well as 1 percent of employee time, is allocated to the effort to make the world cleaner, safer, smarter, and more likely to survive. The input is hybrid, and the projects are hybrid as well, ranging from pure not-for-profit investments to government lobbying campaigns to putting money into companies doing worthwhile things while at the same time seeking profits.

Google hired Dr. Larry Brilliant in 2007 to be executive director of its billion-dollar philanthropic arm. Brilliant, who has since moved on, brought expertise in technology, philanthropy, and public health. Sergey and Larry met with Brilliant weekly to discuss philanthropic efforts.

Google chose six main target initiatives and committed more than $85 million in grants and investments to further these goals:

1. **RE<C** (Renewable Energy Less than Coal): Projects to make other forms of energy cheaper than coal, one of the filthiest sources of energy. Google has made commitments to specific companies working to make solar, wind, and geothermal energy more widely used and economically feasible.

2. **RechargeIT:** Seven different projects aimed at making hybrid, plug-in vehicles a common form of transportation. Google.org planned to invest $10 million in a project that leads to sustainable transportation solutions.

3. **Predict and Prevent:** Four projects that address global threats to health and hunger.

4. **Inform and Empower:** A list of initiatives promoting better education, information, and government participation.
5. **Fuel Growth of Small- and Medium-Sized Enterprises:** A business development effort aimed mostly at rural and poor populations in Africa.
6. **Special Projects and Learning Grants:** A catchall category that overlaps and expands on the other five categories.

Google.org also steps outside its primary focus areas to work on disease eradication, disaster relief, and other immediate needs as they flare up around the world.

GOOGLE AND THE ENVIRONMENT

Look, this is our plan. The sun is going to continue to shine, the wind is going to blow, there's a lot of heat in the earth. Wind, solar, geothermal. If we would just start using that and build a grid that would get that power to where the people are, which is usually not where all that power is, we could solve most of our energy problems. Another thing we think is really important is plug-in hybrids. So you sit there and you go, why plug-in hybrids? It's more economically efficient and uses far less power, hugely, hugely less oil, and by the way, they're built in America. So, for example, in Michigan, which has this huge unemployment problem, you can build the batteries. You can take all those laid-off auto workers and the people who are so terribly affected by this downturn and have them work on things like automobiles and also things like insulation for homes, which is paid back forever.[1]

—*Eric Schmidt, on CNBC's* Mad Money with Jim Cramer

Schmidt elaborated on the point:

We did calculations that said you could save $1 trillion over 22 years by investing in solar, wind and enhanced geothermal, and plug-in hybrids. The sum of those industries are American jobs in states that have high joblessness problems. There is lots and lots of sun, wind and heat in the Earth that is available all the time, whereas we are running out of oil. So this lowers energy prices, increases energy independence and helps to address the climate change issue. It seems like a perfect solution [to U.S. economic problems] if you can pull it off.[2]

"We've seen technologies that we think can really mature into very capable industries that can really generate energy cheaper than coal, and we don't see people talking about that as much as we'd like," said Larry Page.[3]

Eric Schmidt admitted that although the financial and environmental rewards for developing alternative energy sources may be high, so are startup costs:

Clean tech is a little more like the semiconductor busi-ness. The amount of capital required to do it is signifi-cantly higher than in the IT (information technology) businesses I've been involved with. The economics for clean tech may not be the same as Google economics. There are higher capital costs, longer supply chains, inventory risks, more manufacturing, and also the need to build that expertise into companies.[4]

RENEWABLE ENERGY LESS THAN COAL

Google.org finances some of the RE<C initiative, the effort to find cheap electricity-generating power sources. "I know it's a little bit geeky," Larry Page said of the name *renewable energy less than coal.*[5]

Currently there are no energy sources that produce electricity as cheaply as coal. Conversely, few are as dirty as coal. To compete economically, an alternative technol-ogy would need to cost from 1 cent to 3 cents per kilowatt-hour. To make solar energy more competitive, Google's goal is to cut the cost by as much as 50 percent.

At the 2008 Web 2.0 Conference, Larry Brilliant explained: "It's different than pick and shovel invest-ments. It's important that we make money on these investments and for the companies to make a profit. . . . If they don't make money, no one else will and we won't be able to take advantage of capital flows and market forces."

Google has been criticized for investing in RE<C and other initiatives and allocating hundreds of millions of dollars to energy-producing technologies that have no relation to its core business. However, the $45 million investment could eventually both reduce Google's own energy costs and provide a dollar return to the company.

"If we meet this goal, and large-scale renewable deployments are cheaper than coal, the world will have the option to meet a substantial portion of electricity needs from renewable sources and significantly reduce carbon emissions," Larry said. "We expect this would be a good business for us as well."[6]

GEOTHERMAL POWER

"Geothermal, if it works, is better than intermittent producers of solar and wind, and it's also ubiquitous," said Brilliant at the 2008 Web 2.0 Conference.

Larry Page is enthusiastic about the possibility of thermal power's potential: "If you dig deep enough, you get heat. We need to make drilling cheaper."[7] Google. org has sunk more than $10 million into enhanced geothermal energy.

ENERGY FROM THE SEA

Nicola Tesla dreamed of plucking energy from the air; Googlers dream of scooping electrical power from the sea. One of their ideas is to place computer centers on floating barges with an attached power plant to keep the computers running. But it won't be easy. So far, the only sea-related power generators work with wave action as it crashes to shore, and there aren't many of those. In one wave-action project, the whole thing sank into the water off the coast of Oregon. In others, wild seas have broken up the equipment or corroded it beyond use.

ENERGY-EFFICIENT GOOGLEPLEX

Google planned to hire 20 to 30 engineers and experts to pursue its energy conservation ideas using Google's own facilities, which will be the guinea pigs for testing promising technologies.

In 2007, Google announced its intentions to operate in a carbon-neutral environment by the end of the year. In May of that year, Google switched on 9,212 solar panels at Googleplex. Using Google Earth, they are visible from the sky, lined up in neat rows on the rooftops and even atop parking shelters. Googleplex at first had the largest solar installation of any corporate facility, but soon another company surpassed it. However, a Google spokesman says that Googleplex itself wasn't carbon neutral by mid-2008. In fact, the Mountain View campus may never achieve that goal. Some Google facilities around the world may achieve above the goal and others may hit below, but that is okay as long as the company becomes net neutral.

"But just providing energy for Google is not really enough of a goal," Page said. "We really want to provide energy that's cheap enough that it can replace significant amounts of energy that are used today."[8]

~

Thanks to its stated commitment to all things environmental, Google drew flak for Sergey and Larry's personal airplane. The Government Accounting Office (GAO) estimates that global aircraft emissions account for approximately 3.5 percent of the warming generated by human activities. It isn't easy to defend the use of a large plane with few passengers.

When asked about the inefficiencies of the jet, Brin acknowledged it was a problem, but said simply, "It's certainly an issue I've wrestled with."[9]

— Google's Future —

Wall Street analysts and some competitors have a superficial view of Google as a giant college dorm with a fridge stocked with free Odwalla juice.[1]

—Stephen E. Arnold, author and technology consultant

Arnold warns the world not to underestimate Google, its talents, its power, and especially its resolve. If Google has shown us anything so far, it is that Page, Brin, and Schmidt will be smart and aggressive in all aspects of their business.

Even so, Charles O'Reilly, professor of management at Stanford University Graduate School of Business, says, "Gravity affects all organizations and will inevitably affect Google."[2]

Nobody looks to Google for clear signals as to where it is headed. It isn't Google's practice to give guidance. For the longest time, Google claimed to be all about search.

Marc Andreessen, one of the founders of Netscape, said he expects Google to expand everywhere, in both on- and offline computing. "Google is Andy Kaufman—the late comedian. . . . The whole thing with Andy Kaufman was you could never tell when he was joking. Google comes out with a straight face and says, 'We're just going to be a search engine. We're not going to be doing any of this other stuff.' But I am quite sure they are joking."[3]

The array of products Google introduced in the past few years indicates that they were indeed joking. The company website proclaims:

> *What's next from Google? It's hard to say. We don't talk much about what lies ahead, because we believe one of our chief competitive advantages to be surprise. You can always take a peek at some of the ideas that our engineers are currently kicking around by visiting them at Google Labs. Have fun, but be sure to wear your safety goggles.*[4]

The questions ahead for Google are the same as they are for all young companies, especially those that get off to such a swift start. Some of the answers, given in earlier segments, are summarized here:

- **Can the company manage growth?** The answer: So far, profits are good, but investments in future technologies have shown mixed results. "Name any long-term technology bet you can think of," wrote *Time*, "genome-tailored drugs, artificial intelligence, the space elevator—and chances are, there's a team at Googleplex working on an application."[5]

Google has been daring in its pursuit of bright ideas but has had to abandon many of them after investing a large amount of time and money.

- **Can it retain bright and competent employees?** Although Google doesn't release figures on employee attrition, it appears that many early participants have taken their money and left. Yet Google is an interesting place to work and many stay.

- **Can the company deal with intense competitors who shoot for big, successful targets?** This will be the war that never ends. Google has a strong franchise in search technology, but that doesn't mean it will hang onto its lead. Ben Camm-Jones, news editor of *Web User* magazine, points out that competitors will be chasing Google and trying to do search better. "If there's going to be anything, it will be semantic web technology that overtakes Google—if it's a really compelling proposition and if somehow we can shake people out of this belief that Google is the only way to find information on the web."[6]

- **Will the company mature with grace and strength?**
  The world is full of unknowns, but so far Google
  has had luck and brains on its side. There are heavy
  odds that Google will be on our lips and at our
  fingertips for a long time.

The greatest danger to Google's future that Larry and
Sergey face is "the cult of genius." The idea is that they
are so smart they can't make a wrong move. But even
geniuses can make mistakes.

Eric Schmidt isn't so worried about a few mistakes:

*We try to focus on the future. Internally we do talk about
strategy and innovation, not about competitors. It's much
better to look forward to the kinds of things we can do.
Media coverage is all obsessed about winners and losers.
In fact what is really important about technology is you
have the opportunity to redefine the game over and over
. . . and the winner redefines the game.*[7]

Schmidt has tossed out a few clues as to how Google
will define and redefine the future. The company clearly
has engaged Microsoft in a technology war by attacking
it on its own territory. Google has positioned itself to
bring down the software giant by entering Microsoft's
business with cheaper and easier to use products.

Schmidt has said that Google now realizes it can't do
everything alone and hopes to increase its participation

in strategic partnerships, such as the ones it has had with Dell, MySpace, and Adobe.

Additionally, Google will keep a sharp eye on how the economy is going. With all of its strengths, Google was hurt when the 2008 recession arrived. "All of us are vulnerable," Schmidt warned in the fall of 2008. "It's a race between a contraction in advertising, which would affect everybody, and a very positive shift from offline to online."[8]

Formerly a liberal spender, Google will keep a closer eye on expenses because "it's the right thing to do."[9] The company has cut back on free food, limited the number of contractors on board, and trimmed hiring of permanent employees. Google's capital expenditures in the third quarter of 2008 totaled $452 million, an 18 percent decrease from the previous year. As it curbed costs Google's bank account swelled to $14.4 billion in cash, up from $12.7 billion three months earlier.[10]

The recession may be Google's best friend. During a recession many smaller, less hardy competitors drop out of the race. The industry leaders such as Google either acquire the weaker companies or capture their customers. High unemployment rates will help employee retention, since many workers prefer to stay put in hard times, and there aren't many other jobs out there for them to go to. Most convenient of all, recessions let Google do a little housecleaning. The economy becomes easy justification for reviewing the long list of experimental projects and deleting those with marginal chances of contributing to the bottom line.

~

Professor Prabudev Konana, writing about American industry and companies like Google in particular, doesn't claim to know Google's future. But he believes that American high-tech companies will continue to be world leaders:

> The "American Dream" is deep rooted in the American psyche. It is not about owning a three-car garage or gas-guzzling SUVs but it is about innovation and opportunities. U.S. universities are the best in the world for innovation and continue to attract worldwide talent. U.S. firms continue to invest enormous amounts of resources in R&D. All these form the foundation for capitalism to thrive and are not going to go away. . . . There is something in the American spirit— inquisitiveness, individuality, education, risk-taking ability, entrepreneurship, and venture funds—to nurture ideas into great businesses.[11]

ARTIFICIAL INTELLIGENCE

Hidden behind its simple white pages, Google has already created what it says is one of the most sophisticated artificial intelligence systems ever built. In a fraction of a second, it can evaluate millions of variables about its users and advertisers, correlate them with its potential database of billions of ads and deliver the message to which each user is likely to respond.[12]

—*Saul Hansell, writer,* New York Times

During a question-and-answer session after a May 2002 speech at Stanford University, Larry Page said that Google would fulfill its mission only when its search engine was "AI-complete. . . . You guys know what that means? That's artificial intelligence."[13]

Page told the American Association for the Advancement of Science that artificial intelligence was getting a bad rap, but that it was doable and on its way. "My prediction is that when AI happens, it's going to [require] a lot of computation. Not so much clever algorithms. Just a lot of computation. If you look at [a human's] programming, your DNA, it's about 600 megabytes, compressed. So it's smaller than any modern operating system. Smaller than Linux or Windows. . . . So your program algorithms probably aren't that complicated. We have some people at Google who are trying to build artificial intelligence, and to do it at a large scale. . . . I don't think it's that far off."[14]

Like humans, AI learns from experience and logic: "The system can use all the signals available," explained

Jeff Huber, Google's vice president for engineering, "and the system itself learns the correlations between them."[15]

Page explained:

Artificial intelligence would be the ultimate version of Google. So we have the ultimate search engine that would understand everything on the Web. It would understand exactly what you wanted, and it would give you the right thing. That's obviously artificial intelligence, to be able to answer any question, basically, because almost everything is on the Web, right? We're nowhere near doing that now. However, we can get incrementally closer to that, and that is basically what we work on. And that's tremendously interesting from an intellectual standpoint.[16]

When asked what the perfect search engine would be, Sergey Brin, founder of Google, said, "It would be like the mind of God."[17]

Harvard Professor Nicholas Carr said that it is clear that Google's founders believe that someday there will be intelligence greater than what we think of as human intelligence. "Whether that comes out of all the world's computers networked together, or whether it comes from computers integrated with our brains, I don't know, and I'm not sure that Google knows. But the top executives at Google say that the company's goal is to pioneer that new form of intelligence. And the more closely that they can replicate or even expand how peoples' minds work, the more money they make."[18]

Carr then delivered a warning:

I think if Google's users were aware of that intention, they might be less enthusiastic about the prospect than the mathematicians and computer scientists at Google seem to be. A lot of people are worried what a superior intelligence would mean for human beings. I'm not talking about Google robots walking around and pushing humans into lines. But Google seems intent on creating a machine that's able to do a lot of our thinking for us. When we begin to rely on a machine for memory and decision making, you have to wonder what happens to our free will.[19]

ONWARD TO WEB 3.0

With the speed of instant messaging, the computing world is evolving into its third generation. Web 1.0 was centered on computer software companies that arose in the 1980s and 1990s, such as Microsoft, Oracle, and Lotus. These companies developed software that allowed for use and enhancement of computers and everything inside the computer. These early software programs (which are still around and useful) were produced, reproduced, packaged, and marketed much the way traditional products are.

Following the burst of the dot-com bubble in the fall of 2001, the concept of Web 2.0 emerged. Web 2.0 enterprises, most clearly exemplified by Google, Napster, and Amazon.com, existed only on the Internet. They offered a primary service and, in Google's case, often earned money as an ancillary to that service.

Google CEO Eric Schmidt spoke at the Seoul Digital Forum and was asked to define Web 3.0 by a member of the audience. After first joking that Web 2.0 is only "a marketing term," Schmidt launched into a definition of Web 3.0. He said that while Web 2.0 was based on Ajax techniques of building applications, Web 3.0 would be "applications that are pieced together." The applications will be relatively small and perhaps specialized, the data is "in the cloud," the applications can run on all kinds of devices (PC or mobile), and they are very fast, are easily customized, and are distributed virally (by social networks, e-mail, and so on). Additionally, Schmidt noted that Web 3.0 businesses will find low barriers of entry, yet could wind up with very large companies that work everywhere.

Google's great challenge is to continue to come up with products that offer Internet users what they want and need and that make money in the new environment.

This may not be easy. Google's social networking efforts have yet to contribute much to the bottom line.

Google has introduced a range of products that work in the cloud, including Gmail and its suite of productivity software. One of Google's most apparent Web 3.0 tools was Google Mashup Editor (GME), a Web-based program that allowed individuals and businesses to develop their own Web products, sites, and processes by combining various types of media. GME was in the beta stage but was placed in doubt when Google began trimming its products.

CLOUD COMPUTING

A. J. Johnson, a 12-year-old baseball slugger from La Jolla, California, takes cloud computing for granted. He logs on to the Internet each evening to do much of his homework, accesses and completes his assignments from the Google website, gets feedback from his teacher on earlier work, and sees what lies ahead. He can do his lessons from wherever he has access to the Internet— Mom's house, Dad's house, or even Grandmother's house. He can do it from anywhere, and the dog can't eat it.

Yet there is the possibility that the cloud may eat it, or at least make it inaccessible for a certain length of time. A boy can always hope. A. J. and his fellow students aren't the only ones working "in the cloud" these days.

The Lila G. Frederick Pilot Middle School in Boston takes cloud homework a step further. The school has no textbooks. Students pick up laptops at the start of the school day and hand them back at the end. Both teachers and students maintain blogs, staff and parents chat online about the children's work, and assignments are turned in using an electronic "drop box" on the school's website.[20]

What is *cloud computing?* "If you can walk into any library or Internet café and sit down at any computer, not caring what operating system or browser you're using and access a service, that service is cloud based," explained author George Reese.[21]

Google has hailed cloud computing as the future of the Internet and an area in which it will excel. Michael Lorenc, a Google sales and operations manager, spoke to a group of students about computing in the future. "We believe that part of the big innovation, the big new idea, will be cloud computing," he said. "This is because young people coming up, those under 24 years old, have specific expectations regarding the role the Internet plays in their lives."[22]

- They want to have community at the center of their Internet experience.
- They want information to be mobile.
- They expect to be in control of the content they consume and disseminate.[23]

It is estimated that by 2013 at least one-fifth of information technology work will be done online, perhaps never saved on a computer hard drive or portable storage device. By 2019, 50 percent of high school courses will be taught on the cloud.[24]

Cloud computing is quickly replacing much of that data formerly stored on corporate and personal computers. Many of Google's applications, such as its calendar, spreadsheets, and presentation software, are used at home, school, or the office, but reside on Google's own computers.

To Eric Schmidt, this makes a lot of sense. "The basic argument is, if you think about it, it would be better for you to have all the data and all the applications that you use on a server somewhere, and then whatever computer or device you're near you would be able to use," said Schmidt. "Let's say you have a PC or a Mac at home and at the office, and you have a BlackBerry and a portable and so forth and so on. You're constantly moving files around. What happens if you drop your ThinkPad and break it?"

It's just a better model to have the computation and the applications use what we call a cloud, somewhere in the Internet. I, among other people, have been talking about this for 15 years, well before Google was founded. It turned out to be really hard to pull off. But

now finally these broadband networks are fast enough
that you can actually do it. You just don't need to
always have everything on your local computer.[25]

The *cloud* is a controversial buzzword that still frightens some companies, especially large operations that
want, need, or think they need full control over their
data. They worry that if the provider company goes belly
up their data may disappear along with the provider.
There could be hackers, and what if the system goes
down at a critical time for their business? They wonder
if their intellectual property or proprietary information
is safe stored online. Failures do happen.

Newer, smaller operations, however, are finding
cloud computing so cheap, easy, and portable that they
overlook or find ways to protect against the uncertainties. "Any start-up that doesn't use cloud computing
right now is at a competitive disadvantage," claims Tien
Tzuo, founder of the online billing company Zuora.[26]

In fact, cloud computing isn't as exotic or rare as it may
sound. Ten years ago, to do anything on a computer you
needed to buy and install software. Not anymore; e-mail
in boxes is stored online, or in the cloud, rather than on a
personal computer. Services that store photographs and
social networking sites also are cloud-based. Amazon has
long offered pay-as-you-use business services through its

website. Microsoft offers software to use online, as does Apple. Both companies allow users to back up their files online.

Google's cloud computing power arises from the founders' early lack of funds. Larry and Sergey had to scrounge all the PCs they could find and link them together. It worked so well they still do it the same way. The company continues to rely on a massive linked network of small computers to serve customers. The advantage of Google's server farms is that they are scattered around the world and provide backup for one another. If one computer in the mix goes out, it usually doesn't bring down the system. Employees just switch the defunct one out with a new one.

As far back as 2006, experts guessed that Google had as many as one million machines running on Linux, processing queries.[27] Although Google doesn't share that type of information, the number of machines definitely is much larger now, giving Google the strength, depth, and breadth to handle its users' wishes to operate in the cloud.

It all sounds remarkably convenient, but as some users suspect, the plan isn't perfect yet. There are weaknesses, and Google has acknowledged its own susceptibility to error: "Our systems are vulnerable to damage or interruption from earthquakes, terrorist attacks, floods, fires, power loss, telecommunications failures, computer viruses, computer denial of service or other attempts to harm our system, and similar events."[28]

Indeed, Google has experienced service interruptions, such as the one in November 2003, when about 20 percent of Google's customers were without service for about 30 minutes. In 2008, its Gmail service went out for several hours on several days. This alarmed many users, especially those who hoped to engage in cloud computing. But Eric Schmidt shrugged the whole thing off. "That was just a screw up," he explained.[29]

His casual reaction may be annoying to those who needed to perform crucial work during the downtime, but seldom is their cloud information permanently lost. Google has made many computer users accustomed to instant gratification. Like privacy, it's not always there.

YOUTUBE

What do Internet users love more than Google? Surely the answer is YouTube. If you want to check out Alaska Governor Sarah Palin's press conference at a turkey farm, or if you want to hear Will.i.am's stirring "Yes we can" video or are willing to view society in its funniest and rawest form, YouTube is for you.

The leader in online video, YouTube attracts 100 million people each week to access its inventory of five billion videos. YouTube provides a variety of things to watch, even several hours a day of 2008 Olympic coverage on its own dedicated channel.

Part of the fun of YouTube is the chance for fame. People post homemade videos, some of them crude and others—such as the hyperactive character Fred and fashionista William Sledd—quite clever.

Juan Man (not his real name) described himself as aimless and friendless when he strolled into a Sydney, Australia, shopping center holding a sign offering free hugs to anyone who cared to have one. When a video of his hugging escapades was uploaded on YouTube, he became a global sensation. "One week I was washing dishes in Sydney, the next week I was on the Oprah Winfrey Show," he said. "I have friends, I have a fiancée, I have a purpose. And I have never washed dishes since. Unless they were my own, of course."[30]

Much of the content of YouTube, unfortunately, has been commandeered from people and companies that earn their livings producing it. These producers are less than happy at finding their video and audio content free on the Internet. Their displeasure has led to some well-publicized court cases, such as Viacom's $1 billion lawsuit against YouTube for "massive intentional copyright infringement," which is still making its way through the legal system. (For more on that, go to the section "Lawsuits Everywhere" in the chapter "Google Grows Up.")

In 2006, Google paid $1.76 billion to acquire YouTube, based on the popularity of the site and its potential as an advertising machine. So far, YouTube hasn't delivered the goods. By 2008, its revenues were only about $200 million, disappointing considering the number of people using the site. One of the problems is that YouTube cannot legally sell ads that are based on or run with copyrighted material, such as news clips or material from Viacom.

Eric Schmidt keeps promising that sales at YouTube will jump once Google finds the right way to attract people to its advertisements. Schmidt has suggested that the perfect commercial approach at YouTube is "the holy grail."[31] The person who finds an effective way to capitalize on YouTube will have discovered a great treasure.

THE GOOGLE PHONE

Eric Schmidt was asked what he saw as the next big thing in technology: "Mobile, mobile, mobile—it's probably the most wide open space out there right now."[32]

Wearing in-line rollerblades, flaunting their usual junior-high hair cuts, Larry and Sergey stepped out in front of the New York media in the fall of 2008 to introduce Google's long-awaited G1 phone, a handheld multitasking device that competes with Apple's iPhone (for which, not surprisingly, Google provides some software). Google itself brought out the first G1 Android phone but also is franchising the technology to T-Mobile, Sony Ericsson, and other phone companies that wish to market it.

The mobile-phone market is highly competitive and crowded with such weighty players as Research in Motion Ltd., Nokia, Qualcomm, and Apple. Google is a latecomer into the phone software market, but Google goes where the money is. The large number of combatants on the field isn't a problem for them, since Google has the cash to hold on until competition and the economy sort themselves out.

$$\sim$$

What is an android? It is a robot that resembles a human, generally both in appearance and behavior. *Android* also is the given name of the platform on which Google built its G1 phone. Google's Android is a powerful pocket computer, the first complete, open, and free mobile-device platform.

Google did not create Android. It acquired the company in 2005, heralding Google's entry into the mobile-software market. It then turned Android into the Open Handset Alliance, inviting other companies and developers to freely add adaptations and applications.

Android was built atop Apache open-source software because, as Google says on its website,

> *The Apache license allows manufacturers and mobile operators to innovate using the platform without the requirement to contribute those innovations back to the open source community. Because these innovations and differentiated features can be kept proprietary, manufacturers and mobile operators are protected from the "viral infection" problem often associated with other licenses.*[33]

The goal was to come up with flexible, stretchable software that would make using the Internet as smooth on a mobile phone as it is on a computer. "We're not building a phone, we're building a Linux-based OS (operating system), which is likely to be quite different from the iPhone," Schmidt said.[34]

The Google/Android website expanded on Schmidt's remark:

> *But there's more to the Android story. Not only does it allow all applications open access to the phone's functionality; the platform itself will also be open. The Open Handset Alliance has announced its intention to open source the entire Android platform by the end of the year [2008]. Along with the other members of the Alliance, we hope that Android can provide a meaningful*

contribution to all players in the mobile ecosystem: the developers, the wireless carriers, the handset manufacturers, etc. Everyone will be free to adopt and adapt the technology as they see fit. By doing so, we hope that users will get better, more capable phones with powerful Web browsers and access to a rich catalogue of innovative mobile applications.[35]

The platforms may be free for development, but the G1 phone is not. It is priced at just slightly less than Apple's expensive iPhone. Google has set the value of the phone at around $400.

The G1 is a bulky little beast with an awkward slide-out keyboard, but it is a great toy for those who enjoy playing with their cell phones: Sergey likes it because "It's just very exciting for me as a computer geek to be able to have a phone that I can play with and modify and innovate upon, just like I have with computers in the past."[36]

What's the phone like? In the summer of 2008, Google released a software development kit (SKF) that programmers could use to create mobile-phone applications for the company's new Android platform. They then offered the Android Developer's Challenge to get the applications rolling in.

To make the challenge more alluring, the company promised cash prizes ranging from $25,000 to $275,000—up to a total of $1 million—to developers whose applications were chosen by a panel of judges. More than 1,700 applications were developed.[37]As a result, the Google phone has some nifty applications, although some of them may be entertaining for only 10 or 15 minutes. For example, Google likes to show a Googler tossing the phone into the air and catching it, with the phone reporting exactly how long the toss and catch took.[38] The phone will measure a person's carbon footprint on the earth and give tips on how to put less strain on nature. Owners can download software allowing them to scan the bar code of a product and comparison shop on the Internet.

The phone comes with the usual services such as camera, maps, e-mail, and instant messaging. But there is a catch: It has the Google strap attached to it. Users must sign up for a Gmail account to use the phone and its features. There is, of course, a purpose for that. The Gmail leash allows Google to create a unique identifier for each customer that can be used to target ads to the phone user. "That's why they did Android," explained Roger Entner, senior vice president of Nielsen AIG, "to help satisfy Google's need for ad revenues."[39]

WHITE SPACES

Larry Page was ecstatic when the Federal Communications Commission (FCC) voted to open up an unused broadcast television spectrum for other types of broadcasts:

We will soon have Wi-Fi on steroids, since these spec-trum signals have much longer range than today's Wi-Fi technology and broadband access can be spread using fewer base stations resulting in better coverage at lower cost. And it is wonderful that the FCC has adopted the same successful unlicensed model used for Wi-Fi, which has resulted in a projected 1 billion Wi-Fi chips being produced this year.[40]

White spaces are the unused broadcast spectrums that sit between television channels and which likely can be used for high-speed wireless transmission.

Google lobbied fervently in Washington, D.C. and on the Internet for such a change. Google gathered more than 13,000 signatures supporting its point of view through its "Free the Airways" campaign.

Other major companies, including Microsoft and Motorola, joined Google in the crusade. Page, however, was point man on the six-year effort. A Google spokes-person said that Page had a "personal interest" in the matter. We don't know for sure what the personal inter-est was, except that Page sees white spaces as a poten-tial medium for advertising.

Larry acknowledged that his interest in expanded access to white spaces wasn't entirely altruistic. Google stands a chance of expanding its advertising revenues 20 to 30 percent thanks to the use of white spaces.

The FCC approval was evidence of the influence Google has gained in Washington, D.C.[41]

Why are the white spaces of such interest to computer and Internet companies? White spaces are another free infrastructure, much like the Internet, on which a business can be built or expanded. Powerful cell phone companies had been pressuring the government to auction off white space licenses to the highest bidder, making it easier for the established, wealthiest companies to control Wi-Fi usage.

Larry said that the development of Wi-Fi itself shows what entrepreneurial scientists can do if they get a chance. "We all use Wi-Fi all the time. Wi-Fi was an accident. It was a useless spectrum. It was put in the license regime. Engineers came along and worked on it and made it better and now we have excellent Wi-Fi."

But, he said, Wi-Fi as it is distributed now has limitations, especially in the speed and distance it will travel. White spaces offer the possibility of allowing lower-cost devices and can serve well in rural areas where broadband isn't available in other ways. "I'm really, really excited about it."[42] And, he noted, the expansion of white space comes "at no cost to anyone in the country."

Still, there were worries about interference with television and wireless microphones. Several early tests of white spaces devices didn't turn out well, and some believe that Wi-Fi in white spaces just won't work.

The FCC's Office of Engineering and Technology released a report on July 31, 2007, with results from its investigation of two preliminary devices. The report concluded that the devices did not reliably sense the presence of television transmissions or other preexisting users. For that reason, the devices were not deemed acceptable for use in their current state, and no further testing was thought to be necessary.

However, a month later, Microsoft filed a document with the FCC in which its engineers described a meeting that they had with representatives from the Office of Engineering and Technology. The Microsoft crew showed the FCC results from their tests done with identical prototype devices and using identical testing methods. Microsoft did detect other signals and the equipment performed exactly as expected. In the presence of FCC engineers, the Microsoft engineers disassembled the device that the FCC had tested and found that its scanner had been damaged and did not work properly, which explained the FCC's inability to know when channels were being used.

Eventually it was determined that sensing technology was effective but was not foolproof in dealing with interference. When coupled with geolocation technology, though, interference was limited to a manageable level. With the addition of the GPS information, the white spaces were released for use.

Google had tried unsuccessfully to get into the Wi-Fi business before, starting with a citywide system for San Francisco. That partnership with Earthlink fell apart. An Earthlink executive was quoted as saying that it was a "good idea but a bad business."[43]

Larry insisted that opening the white spaces benefitted everyone: It was the right thing for the FCC to do. By making the Internet easier, cheaper, and available in remote areas, it would put more people on the right side of the Internet divide.

As an engineer, I was also really gratified to see that the FCC decided to put science over politics. For years the broadcasting lobby and others have tried to spread fear and confusion about this technology, rather than allow the FCC's engineers to simply do their work.[44]

The Dominant — Power in the Industry?

It's Google's world. We just live in it.[1]

—Chris Tolles, vice president of marketing, Topix Inc.

I think, therefore I Google.[2]

—David Smith, columnist, The Guardian

Blogger Paul Ford published an article anticipating the future: "How Google Beat Amazon and eBay to the Semantic Web." He illustrated the story with a rough-cut cartoon of a giant robot standing on the globe and declaring, "I am Googlebot, I control Earth." Most readers saw the cartoon as a slap at Google, except for those who worked at Google. They contacted Ford requesting that they be allowed to put the doodle on t-shirts. Ford said no, but the cartoon popped up on walls, bulletin boards, and desks all over Google offices.[3]

Sounds like Google is full of itself, doesn't it? A generous amount of hubris is essential to being a Silicon Valley leader. "There is a certain 'we can do this' arrogance in Silicon Valley," admits Marc Tarpenning, software engineer and one of the founders of Tesla Motors. "But all entrepreneurs need a bit of that because if you really understood how difficult this stuff is, you would just never do it."[4]

While it is obvious that Google rules the kingdom of search, even the experts can't get a handle on the ramifications of Google's dominance. *BusinessWeek* wrote in 2007 that the company's data-gathering capability worries many people. Technology historian George Dyson, who wrote *Darwin Among the Machines: The Evolution of Global Intelligence*, believes Google could pose a national defense problem simply by virtue of its huge warehouse of data.

> *"That much money and power concentrated in one place can be dangerous," says Dyson, who sometimes advises the Defense Department on potential threats. While he doesn't think Google yet represents such a menace, he raises a more obvious concern: Google's vast network, now a substantial piece of the Internet itself, is "very*

*quickly becoming vital national security infrastructure."
Should anything happen to the company, he says,
through market forces, terrorist attacks on server farms,
or something else, that could compromise national
defense.*[5]

Esther Dyson, a venture capitalist who has a close relationship with Google, wrote:

*The danger lies in the concentration of information—
arguably a concentration of power—that Google represents. Google doesn't merely point users to existing
information on the Web; it also collects information
that it doesn't share about its users' behavior. If you
can use patterns in Google searches to track flu out-
breaks and predict a movie's commercial prospects,
can you also use it to forecast market movements or
even revolutions?*[6]

Or even how to manipulate and influence searchers to
think and act in certain ways? The thing about Google
is most people don't realize how much it knows about
them and how readily it can tailor response, information, advertisements, and so on, to sway their thinking.
The very nature of propaganda and influence is that
people tend to be unaware of how they are being
worked over.

Google appears to be an unstoppable online giant, capable of growing at the same speed that the Internet grows. On a corporate level, Google challenges everyone even remotely near it. In 2008, it came out with the GPhone to confront Apple's iPhone, and Chrome to defy Microsoft, and then launched Knol, a peer-reviewed encyclopedia to undercut Wikipedia.

Andy Grove, former CEO of Intel, described Google as a company "on steroids, with a finger in every industry."

"Microsoft's power," Grove observed, "was intra-industry, Google's power is shaping what's happening to other industries."[7]

Google's Marissa Mayer insists the company's power is legitimate and well-deserved: "Our influence comes from the end-users and the trust that we've built with them. If we stop putting their needs first, that will stop."[8]

Esther Dyson agreed, arguing that people are always free to use another search engine if they think something unhealthy is going on. Dyson concluded,

A Google that is accountable to its users—searchers, advertisers, investors, and governments—is likely to be a better outfit that does more good in today's relatively open market. In short, there is no regulatory system that I trust more than the current messy world of conflicting interests. Whatever short-term temptations it faces—to manipulate its search results, use private information, or throw its weight around—Google, it is clear, could lose a lot by succumbing to them in a world where its every move is watched.[9]

Dyson's reasoning is similar to comments regarding the credit and financial services industries prior to their 2008 catastrophes. In other words, she was saying the market, competitors, and customers keep the system honest and efficient. The recent failure of that concept convinced most Americans that while a free-market system has a crucial creativity and energy, every industry needs some guiding principles and oversight.

~

Even though most curbs to Google's power have come from the courts, it has been disciplined by the free-market system.

Each year, thousands of eBay enthusiasts trek to Boston for the online consignment store's sellers' convention. In 2007, Google showed up, too, staging a "Let Freedom Ring" party to protest eBay's refusal to let merchants use Google Checkout. "We were not pleased by this notion of the Google Checkout party and the marketing around it, I will tell you that," said eBay CEO Meg Whitman.[10]

Checkout is a direct competitor with eBay's payment system, PayPal, which eBay acquired in 2002. PayPal is by far the online payment leader, with more than 143 million user accounts worldwide. A gem of an acquisition, PayPal has been growing faster than eBay's core auction and shopping business. Rajiv Dutta, who oversees PayPal, said, "I am convinced PayPal is one day going to be bigger than eBay."[11]

"We're defending ourselves aggressively with PayPal," Whitman said. "That is one of our core businesses. We're not going to let that go away to someone who'd kind of like to be in the business."[12]

As it happens, eBay also is among Google's largest advertisers, spending tens of millions of dollars a year on keyword advertising. Whitman promptly canceled all of its U.S. Google ads for more than a week. Google got the message and canceled its "freedom" party just as promptly.

GOOGLE, MICROSOFT, AND THE INTERNET CIVIL WAR

In 2003, Sergey Brin told the *New York Times* that he wouldn't knowingly challenge Microsoft. "Netscape antagonized Microsoft," he said. "We are not putting ourselves in the bull's eye as Netscape did."[13] A year later, in its IPO prospectus, Google wrote, "We face significant competition from Microsoft and Yahoo!."

At first, Google insisted that it had no fight to pick with Microsoft. That gradually changed. In 2006, Eric Schmidt was asked who Google's primary competitors were:

Well, today we compete with Yahoo! all the time because they are the other company that has a targeted advertising network. And Microsoft continues to claim to enter the [search] market, but we really haven't seen them yet, they're just getting started. I'm sure eventually Microsoft will be a competitor. So it's really those three companies, Google, Yahoo! and Microsoft.[14]

"We just see the history of [Microsoft] behaving anti-competitively and . . . not playing fair," said Brin. "So I think we want to . . . look at the area where that power can be abused."[15]

Google soon took the offense, and a bitter rivalry escalated between the companies. Not only did Google throw the gauntlet down on practically every path Microsoft was following, they opened a recruiting office not far from Microsoft's headquarters in Redmond, Washington, and made raids on Microsoft's talent pool. But more significantly, it offered Google Apps, free online productivity software similar to Microsoft Office. Then came Gmail, and in 2008, Google launched Chrome, the free browser that challenged one of Microsoft's most lucrative products, Internet Explorer.

Microsoft Chairman Steve Ballmer became so angry over losing key employees to Google, that he declared war: "I'm going to fucking kill Google."[16]

When asked by CNBC's Jim Cramer whether Microsoft should worry about Google's cloud computing, Eric Schmidt shot back, "I never worry about Microsoft."[17]

Rupert Murdoch would agree with Schmidt that Google doesn't need to worry. "They've got so much money they don't know what to do with it," Murdoch said. "They keep employing people, testing new ideas, trying things, putting out new free applications, relying on advertising for income. Which makes them unbelievably, unbelievably competitive with what Microsoft would charge for the same things."[18]

Wired magazine wrote that the war between Microsoft and Google is "a classic battle between youth and experience, or as Google likes to believe, good and evil."[19]

Just 20 or so years earlier, Microsoft was the whiz-kid company—young, vigorous, and cocky. In time, Microsoft lost the luster of the new. Then some corporate actions, such as the way it crushed competitor Netscape, made it the scourge of Silicon Valley. Many people were pleased that there was now a company that could go nose-to-nose with Microsoft and hold its own.

Microsoft, as could be expected, fired back at Google's advance into its territory. When the test version of Internet Explorer (IE) 8 came out, it appeared to have a feature that might block Google's targeted advertising. For a company that relies almost entirely on Web advertising for its revenues, and considering how pervasive the IE browser is, that could be a powerful strike.

THE BATTLE OF YAHOO!

The 2008 fight over Yahoo! turned the intense rivalry between the two companies into open warfare. It escalated into a battle of biblical proportions. It was a war for power and control in the digital world—the former David versus the former Goliath—Google against Microsoft.

As early as 2006, Yahoo!'s financial results began to weaken, largely due to competition from Google. Google was going after Yahoo!'s core businesses with its Gmail, Google Video, personals, and other features within Google Base.

Late that year, Microsoft and Yahoo! began discussions about hooking up, either in partnerships or by acquisition. Yahoo! sent Microsoft packing, saying the time wasn't right. The situation at Yahoo! continued to deteriorate, and in January 2008, Ballmer made a $44 billion, $31-per-share offer to acquire Yahoo!.

Yahoo! had many attributes that Microsoft found attractive, especially its search technology and its ownership of Overture. Yahoo! balked at Microsoft's offer, and in May, Microsoft upped the ante to $47.5 billion, or $33 per share. Again, Yahoo! Chairman Jerry Yang refused, saying that Yahoo! was worth at least $37 per share.

By now, shareholders, especially investor Carl Icahn, were upset with Yang. The battle for control of Yahoo!

eventually prompted several pension funds to sue the Yahoo! board for rebuffing the Microsoft offer. Yang's actions also pitted billionaire investor Icahn against Bill Miller, Legg Mason chief investment officer and CEO. Icahn initially demanded that Yahoo! accept Microsoft's purchase offer, but eventually he made peace with Yang and, with two other representatives, joined the board of directors. Miller sided with Yahoo!, but left the door open for Microsoft to make another try.

In June, Google put a dog in the fight when it offered Yahoo! a search partnership to bolster its earnings. The deal was expected to yield Yahoo! $800 million in annual advertising revenues. "There's no question in our view that an independent Yahoo! is better," said Schmidt, adding that it "will provide more competition in search and other advertising markets, in particular in display advertising."[20]

"Microsoft has a long history of having deals that look quite good and end up looking not so good when you read the fine print," Schmidt said.[21]

The *Financial Times* of London didn't like the smell of Google's offer. The newspaper said the deal demonstrated Google at its worst, "a combination of naïve insouciance and thinly veiled scheming."

The insouciance was shown by Sergey Brin, who earlier this year blithely told a group of reporters (including this one) that the alliance was all about helping out old friends. After all, Yahoo!'s Jerry Yang and David Filo had lent the Google founders a hand when they were just starting out, and anyway, their companies' cultures were very similar.

The scheming was the obvious ulterior motive here, to block Microsoft. Asked about how they set corporate strategy, Google executives always deny they have such thoughts: Everything they do is for the benefit of the customers. But this partnership betrayed one of Google's most powerful psychoses, its paranoia about Microsoft.[22]

Within months, it became clear that the U.S. Justice Department and Canadian regulators would not approve the Google–Yahoo! deal, since it gave the two companies 90 percent of the paid search market. Advertisers also were up in arms about the alliance, saying it would give Google and Yahoo! too much influence over pricing and other online advertising issues.

Google pulled out in early November. The company's chief legal officer David Drummond explained: "We're of course disappointed that this deal won't be moving ahead. But we're not going to let the prospect of a lengthy legal battle distract us from our core mission. That would be like trying to drive down the road of innovation with the parking brake on."[23]

At the same time, the economy and the financial market kets went into a slide. Yahoo!'s share price fell off a cliff. Yahoo! went back to Microsoft, hat in hand, but it was too late. CEO Steve Ballmer was no longer interested. "We made an offer, we made another offer, and it was clear that Yahoo! didn't want to sell the business to us and we moved on," Ballmer said. "We are not interested in going back and re-looking at an acquisition. I don't know why they would be either, frankly. They turned us down at $33 a share."[24]

The skirmish ended with Google the clear victor. Microsoft was stopped from acquiring Yahoo! and building a fortress in the search business. Yahoo! was so shattered that by the end of the year, its share price had declined 48 percent. From a 52-week high of $30.25, Yahoo! ended the year at about $12 per share. From a company Microsoft was willing to buy for more than $47 billion, Yahoo! ended with market capitalization of $17.8 billion. Yahoo! announced it would lay off 10 percent of its workforce. Once the second leading search engine, Yahoo! no longer presented much of an opposition to Google.

~

While Google certainly has shaken Microsoft's confidence on the search and advertising fronts, Microsoft reigns supreme in other areas. A writer for *Forbes* asked this question: "Have you heard of any big companies that have ditched Microsoft Office and switched to the free Google Apps? Me neither. . . . Google has failed on that front because its apps simply aren't that compelling."[25]

~

The war is not over, although most experts figure Google is in the lead. The prize is big, and it will be a fight worth watching. "Microsoft . . . continues to try to catch a runaway freight train with Google, and the reality is Microsoft's tried organically so many times and really has little to show for it," said Citigroup Global Markets Inc. software analyst Brent Thill.[26]

"They [Google] are the company that is going to have more influence and more control over the structure of the world information industry than any other," said David B. Yoffie, a professor at the Harvard Business School. "The right way to think about Google is, they are the next Microsoft."[27]

GATES ON GOOGLE

Bill Gates admitted that Google "kicked our butts" on search-engine technology. He later announced that Microsoft would launch its own search engine.[28] "Google is still, you know, perfect," Gates said in 2005. "The bubble's still floating. You should buy their stock at any price. We had a ten-year period like that."[29]

~

Microsoft was at the height of its attempt to acquire Yahoo! when Gates was asked how he felt about the fact that Google was invented at the William Gates Building at Stanford University. Gates began his usual boxing shuffle when asked a question, bobbing and glancing up, down, and sideways. "Competition is a good thing," he said (pause, shuffle). "On the other hand, nobody's doing a very good job of competing with Google right now."[30]

The next day, to Google's delight, Microsoft abandoned its bid to purchase Yahoo!.

~

When Gates heard that Google agreed to Chinese censorship rules so it could attain access to the lucrative Chinese market, he chortled that perhaps the company motto should become, "Do less evil."[31]

Conclusion

Within the last seven days, Google has altered and augmented my perceptions of tulips, mind control, Japanese platform shoes, violent African dictatorships, 3-D high-definition wallpaper, spicy chicken dishes, tiled hot tubs, biological image-processing schemes, Chihuahua hygiene, and many more critical topics. Clearly, thanks to Google, I am not the man I was seven days ago.[1]

—*John Gaeta, visual effects supervisor,*

the Matrix *trilogy*

Imagine doing that for someone? Imagine doing that for 90 million people a day? Larry Page and Sergey Brin can say they have changed the world. Their story, and that of Google, makes one of the most interesting tales of this century or the best "so far," as Homer Simpson would say. And, admits Brin, "the number-one factor that has contributed to our success over the past seven years has been luck."[2]

It has been a dramatic journey from when Page and Brin celebrated milestones by going to Burger King for hamburgers and when they played roller hockey in the parking lot with employees. Those were the good-old-days. Google has moved on to the good new days and to a time when it has enormous responsibility to the public, to employees, and to shareholders.

"There are people who think we are plenty full of ourselves right now, but from inside at least, it doesn't look that way," said Craig Silverstein, Google's technology director and its first employee. "I think what keeps us humble is realizing how much further we have to go."[3]

Google also presents one of the most perplexing paradoxes of our time. We love Google, we use it obsessively, we bare our souls to it. The information makes us healthier, wealthier, and wiser. Information is the underpinning of personal and political freedom.

On the other hand, we don't understand how Google really works. It feels as if it knows too much about us and has too much control over us. We are suspicious of it. The whole process of search and search-related advertising challenges age-old concepts of personal privacy. When it comes to property rights, Google seems to have the attitude, "What's mine is mine; what's yours is mine."

"As a corporation," wrote *BusinessWeek*, "it's often a cipher, its intentions and methods concealed by algorithms that look impenetrable and impersonal. Yet the search engine and the blockbuster business built atop it utterly depends upon millions of people sharing through searches their most intimate desires, and upon thousands of businesses willing to open their data storehouses to feed Google's voracious digital maw."[4]

The question that most people ask about the company is, "Do they really do no evil?" It is their oft-stated intention *not* to do evil, and very likely they don't do evil on purpose. But the Google guys are human, and Google is a complex business. Different people have different definitions of *evil*. In its dozen years of existence, Google has changed its own definition of right and wrong. Originally, the founders refused to offer horoscopes, financial advice, or chat. Horoscopes were considered bogus, financial advice often suspect, and chat superfluous. They originally claimed not to accept pornography advertisements, but then such ads would mysteriously appear. Those ideals have long gone by the wayside.

Ah, well, evil happens.

Writing in Canada's *The Globe and Mail* newspaper, Matt Harley and Grant Robertson insist that "Google is a work in progress, and always will be. The Mountain View, Calif., Company exists in a state of perpetual beta, and it's a corporate philosophy that has helped drive the company's seeming boundless innovation."[5]

As long as the company continues with high profitability and outstanding growth, it can get away with a lot of missteps and mistakes. But once those two measurements of success lag, it will deal with the same harsh judgments other mature companies must face. In fact, some of those criticisms have begun.

Trip Chowdhry, a senior analyst at Global Equities Research, claims that being the king of search won't be enough to sustain Google over the long term: "Name me anything they've been successful in besides search," Chowdhry asks. "I think the board and management of Google needs a total overhaul."[6]

Certainly investors have signaled their doubts about Google. The stock started 2008 off strong with shares hovering above $690—slightly below the all-time high of $747.24 as of November 2007. But as 2008 progressed, the company's stock plunged 56 percent, partly because of fears that its revenue growth would tank. Google's core business has in fact slowed, but held up reasonably well during the 2008 to 2009 financial turmoil.

Despite the legitimate fears, Google remains a stable organization and a trusted brand with a strong franchise. The number of searches done on Google grows every month.

Its ad revenues have also been on a fast track. In 2007, Google outstripped every other media company, whether it was the Web, TV, print, or radio. Google's ad revenues outstripped 17 major media businesses, including News Corp, Time Warner Cable, Viacom, Yahoo!, Microsoft, AOL, the *New York Times*, and CBS Radio. Online ad revenue for these 17 companies grew 9 percent that year, while total online revenues grew 28 percent. Google's online ad revenues grew 44 percent compared with 15 percent for the combined online ad revenues of Yahoo!, Microsoft, and AOL.[7] Revenue growth declined slightly in 2008 and was expected to slide more in 2009. Still, Google leads its pack and continues to rake in the money. The positive side of the company far, far outweighs the negative.[8]

Eric Schmidt announced a defensive plan for Google but said he was bullish about the economic outlook for Silicon Valley companies.

"This is the sixth or seventh cycle I've seen in Silicon Valley. I think we're better positioned than ever." Then he placed the blame squarely on the area's terrific weather, and Larry Page agreed:

"I don't think there's anywhere else you'd rather be. We're investors in Tesla, for example. It's pretty amazing you can drive an electric car with a 220-mile range. Those are produced here. I don't see those anywhere else in the world."[9]

Silicon Valley is amazing, but before the end of 2008, Google announced it was trimming overhead and laying off much of its 10,000-strong contract workforce. Even Tesla, with its backlog of sales to movie stars and industry moguls, felt the pinch.

Admittedly, Google's survival is anything but guaranteed. The company operates in a quick-changing, highly competitive environment—it is involved in a global scientific and economic boxing match. Yet, if the founders continue to be as cautious and crafty as they have been in the past, they will prosper. "Google will keep pushing the envelope," predicted writer John Battelle. "It's one of the things that seems to make them happy."[10]

LESSONS FROM LARRY AND SERGEY

What can we learn from the Google story?

- **The American dream is alive and well.** It may flicker, it may fade, it may seem far away, but it still beckons us forward. Anything is possible.
- **A high-quality education system is an important incubator.** Thanks to Montessori schools, public schools, great state universities, and Stanford University, the Google guys were able to learn what they needed to know to formulate and develop their ideas. When they arrived at Stanford, they found the knowledge, technology, equipment, and even financing they needed. By then, they were ready

for it. Stanford is an excellent example of how a great university can promote science and business innovation, but there are numerous other examples. Both Microsoft and Facebook were launched on Harvard's computers.

- **Don't focus on the money; focus instead on excellent results.**
- **Have fun.** Others will be more than willing to support you in your work, especially if it is playful and pleasant.
- **Don't be evil—or at least try your best to conduct business in an honest and fair manner.** This one isn't easy, but it's a commendable aspiration.

THE TRAITS OF THOSE WHO CHANGE THE WORLD

I've written about many people who have changed the world with their ideas and actions. These include Bill Gates of Microsoft, Warren Buffett of Berkshire Hathaway, Jack Welch of General Electric, Ted Turner, creator of CNN, Oprah Winfrey, and others. I'm often asked what characteristics these exceptional people have in common.

- Foremost, *they trust themselves* and follow their own ideas. They have intuition, but more important, they listen to that inner voice. *Intuition* is not a supernatural phenomenon. It is a combination of your total knowledge, your experience, your thinking and feeling self, and your present mindset. It can be your automatic pilot.

- *Fresh thinking* is essential. As the world of technology evolves, new problems arise daily. Old problems return to haunt. Bill Gates and Paul Allen did not even think of the past as they worked up the first operating system for the first personal computer. They simply surveyed the challenge and dove for the answer.

- They are *curious*. Larry Page and Sergey Brin continually ask questions and probe the answers to see whether they work.

- They engage their *imagination*. They think of what may be possible. They think big. Imagination is a gift, but it also can be cultivated.

- They are *bold*, sometimes in a brash way, sometimes in a genteel way. They push and poke beyond what others, even their own mentors, have done. They don't hesitate when they know they are right. A strong positive attitude carries them forward, far forward.

Timeline

1955—Eric Emerson Schmidt was born on April 27 in Washington, D.C.

1973—Lawrence Edward Page was born on March 26 in Ann Arbor, Michigan.

Sergey Mikhailovich Brin was born on August 21 in Moscow, Russia.

1979—The Brin family, which included young Sergey, his parents and grandmother, arrived in the United States on October 25.

1995—Larry Page and Sergey Brin met when Brin guided a tour of San Francisco for prospective new Stanford graduate students.

1996—Page and Brin collaborated on Page's BackRub search engine.

The first version of Google is released in August on the Stanford Web. The address: google.stanford.edu. A little over a year later, the search engine left

Stanford servers because it took up too much
bandwidth.

1997—Google.com was registered as a domain name.

The young inventors tried to sell Google through
the venture capital firm of Kleiner Perkins Caufield &
Byers (KPCB). After unsuccessfully pitching the
search engine to all likely buyers, they gave up the
idea of selling.

1998—Google was getting more than 10,000 queries
a day.

Andy Bechtolsheim, a founder of Sun Microsystems,
watched the demo for Google and immediately wrote
a $100,000 check to get the company started. Google
became an official corporation on September 7.

A few weeks after incorporation, Craig Silverstein
became Google's first employee.

PC magazine recognized Google as the search
engine of choice and one of the Top 100 Web Sites for
1998.

1999—After several months of operating out of a rented
bedroom and garage, Google opened its first Palo Alto
office. Later in the year, the company moved to
Bayshore Drive in nearby Mountain View.

Kleiner Perkins Caufield & Byers, in partnership
with Sequoia Capital, provided Google with additional venture capital of $25 million.

Brin and Page finally dropped out of the Stanford graduate studies program.

Omid Kordestani, the company's twelfth employee and its first nonengineer, joined Google as head of global sales. Kordestani is credited with creating the advertising model that led to Google's early and continuing financial glory.

Charlie Ayers, who once cooked for the Grateful Dead, joined Google as its chef.

2000—By mid-year, Google searches had swollen to 18 million per day, and the Google index grew to more than 1 billion documents, making it the largest search engine in the world.

The first ten foreign-language versions of Google.com were released, available in French, German, Italian, Swedish, Finnish, Spanish, Portuguese, Dutch, Norwegian, and Danish. Later in the year, Chinese, Japanese, and Korean languages were added.

Yahoo! selected Google as its default search provider.

Google began selling AdWords, its key-word-related advertising.

2001—Eric Schmidt joined Google as its first chairman and later in the year became chief executive officer.

Google acquired Deja.com's discussion group site UseNet and merged it into Google Groups. This was Google's first acquisition.

"Don't be evil" was first heard in a meeting and later became Google's informal ethical motto.

2002—Larry Page approached his alma mater, the University of Michigan, about scanning their library into Google's cache of pages.

Google announced it would provide search services to AOL.com, Compuserve, and Netscape.

Inspired by the September 11 terrorist attacks, Google News launched with 4,000 news sources.

Froogle shopping services went online. Not much of a success, it later was renamed Google Product Search.

2003—The American Dialect Society voted *google* the most useful word of 2002.

The company acquired Pyra Labs/Blogger.

AdSense went into service for advertisers.

Registration opened for Google's first Code Jam programming competition.

2004—Google moved to its new Mountain View campus, nicknamed Googleplex.

Gmail became available as a free e-mail service.

Google announced it would go public on April 29.

Google went public on Friday, August 13, with an initial public offering price of $85.

Google quietly started digitizing the University of Michigan's library in July. Later in the year, "Google Print for Libraries" project was announced. The project has had several name changes and most lately is called the Print Library Project.

The social networking site Orkut went online.

2005—Google raised another $4.2 billion through a second stock offering.

The company acquired Flickr, the popular photo-sharing website.

Its first lobbyist office opened in Washington, D.C., with a staff of one.

Google Maps, Google Earth, and iGoogle were released.

Urchin (Web traffic metrics) was purchased.

The first Summer of Code took place, a three-month, $2 million program aiming to help computer science students contribute to open source development.

Google Talk went online, a Windows application enabling Gmail users to talk on Instant Message with a friend using a computer microphone and speaker. The service does not require a phone and is free.

2006—The U.S. Justice Department demanded records of millions of search-engine users. Google successfully fended off the demand in court.

Google went live in China.

By purchasing dMarc Broadcasting, a radio advertising company, Google expanded offline activity.

Google (the verb) was added to the *Oxford English Dictionary*.

Google purchased YouTube.

Dr. Larry Brilliant was hired to be the executive director of Google.org, the company's philanthropic arm.

2007—*Fortune* named Google as best company to work for in the United States.

Gmail became available to everyone. Previously, it was available by invitation only.

Street View in Google Maps was launched in five U.S. cities. Later in the year, Sky was initiated inside Google Earth, showing layers for constellations and virtual tours of the galaxies.

Hot Trends began listing the current 100 most active queries, serving as a global subconscious indicating what the masses are thinking about at almost any moment.

Viacom filed $1 billion suit against Google for airing its programs on YouTube without permission or pay.

The $3.2 billion purchase of DoubleClick sparked complaints that Google was becoming too dominant in the advertising industry. Soon after the acquisition, Google laid off 300 DoubleClick employees.

Sergey Brin and Anne Wojcicki were married in the Bahamas.

The first CNN/YouTube debates took place, first between Democratic presidential candidates and later between Republicans.

Google formed the Open Handset Alliance to work on its Android project.

Larry Page and Lucinda Southworth were married on Necker Island in the Caribbean.

The Queen of England launched The Royal Channel on YouTube, the first monarch to establish a video presence this way.

2008—Yahoo! agreed to use some Google ads on its search engine, a controversial agreement that fell under intense public and political scrutiny.

The company bid in the 700 MHz spectrum wireless communication auction.

Google Health became available.

For the first time ever on the Internet, Google provided real-time stock quotes.

Google launched Chrome, its first Web browser.

A satellite with the Google logo was launched from Vandenberg Air Force Base in California. The satellite will provide high-resolution photos for Google's mapping service.

Glossary

Ajax Acronym for *Asynchronous JavaScript and XML*. This is a group of interrelated Web development tools used for creating interactive or rich Internet applications. With Ajax, Web programs can access data without interfering with the display and behavior of the page on the screen.

Algorithm Procedure or formula for solving a problem.

Artificial intelligence (AI) The study and design of machines that can operate like the human mind.

Atomic phrase A phrase that can elicit the most specific, single-idea result.

Beta Software that is released to the public on a trial basis to work out any imperfections before the official version is released. A software program that remains in development.

Blog Short for *Web log*, or a string of journal entries posted on a Web page.

Bot Short for *robot*, a program that automatically searches the Internet looking for information. Google uses two versions of search bots, the Deepbot and Freshbot. Deepbot tries to crawl every link on the Web and index as many pages as possible, whereas Freshbot seeks newly available and updated content and websites.

Captchas An acronym for *completely automated public Turing test to tell computers and humans apart.* Wavy, distorted text used as a security test to thwart mass registration of e-mail accounts (for sending spam mail) and other Web abuses.

Chrome Software lingo for toolbars and task bars that characterize most computer programs. Google named its Internet browser Chrome, after these classic tools.

Clickstream A digital path showing where an Internet user has been. The click of a mouse represents each step on the path.

Cloud computing There are various definitions for this concept. Basically it means that data is not stored or processed on a computer's hard drive. Rather, the user logs on to the Internet for processing and storage.

Folksonomy (tagging) The practice and method of collaboratively creating and managing items, titles, names, or the like, to annotate and categorize content. The Dewey Decimal System, for example, is a folksonomy of books that can be found in a library.

Googlejuice   The number of links or references one website has to other sites. A site with a large number of links has a lot of Googlejuice.

Grok   To understand. The word suggests an intimate and exhaustive knowledge. In the search process, *grokking* means to analyze the pool of information to produce the answer to a search.

Malware   Malicious or harmful software, such as viruses.

Mashup   A digital media file containing a mix of text, audio, and animation; it recombines and tweaks each work to create a derivative work. Mashup music and videos, for example, are a collage of other works.

Metadata   Data about data of any nature in any media. An item of metadata may describe an individual datum, or content item, or a collection of data with multiple content items. Clickstreams are a form of metadata.

Network neutrality   A philosophy that prevents Internet providers from interfering with Web content based on the source of ownership.

Optimizers   Search-engine optimizers promise website managers that they can get their site high placement in search results all over the Web. This is done by clever use of key words and other tricks that distort results.

PDA   Acronym for *personal digital assistant*, such as the multipurpose iPhone or Blackberry mobile telephone.

PDF Created by Adobe, *Portable Document Formatting* captures formatting information from a variety of desktop publishing applications, making it possible to send formatted documents and allowing them to appear on the computer user's monitor or printer as they were meant to be.

Petabyte (PB) Derived from the mathematical/scientific prefix *peta-*; a unit of information or computer storage equal to one quadrillion bytes, or 1,000 terabytes.

Podcast Digital media files distributed over the Internet for viewing on a computer or downloading and playback on portable media players.

Poking In computing, this refers to the storage of a value in a memory address, typically to modify the behavior of a program or to cheat at a video game.

SEO *Search-engine optimization* is the work of improving the volume and quality of traffic to a website from search engines. Often, the sooner a site appears in the search results, or the higher the rank, the more searchers will click on that site. SEO also targets different types of search, such as image search, local search, and industry-specific searches.

Scale As in, "It was a good idea, but it didn't scale." In Silicon Valley, this usually refers to the question of whether a product or service is economically viable. To *scale* means the idea or product can successfully move to a much larger model. It originates with the concept *economies of scale*. This is the idea that the efficiency of production of goods increases as the number of goods being produced increases. Thus, the average cost of producing a good will diminish as each additional good is produced, since the fixed costs are shared over an increasing number of goods.

Semantic Web   The extension of the World Wide Web that enables people to share content beyond the boundaries of applications and websites. The semantic Web is a simple organization that gives Web users easy and logical access to a huge amount of information.

SMS   *Short Message Service*, or text messaging between mobile phones. SMS text messaging is said to be the most widely used data application on the planet, with 2.4 billion users, or 74% of all mobile-phone subscribers exchanging text messages on their phones.

Social networking   Websites that allow people to share ideas, information, and images and to form networks with friends, family, or other like-minded individuals.

Sticky   Any trick or device that keeps an Internet user at a specific site.

Tagging   Naming an image, file, or something on the Internet. It needs a name before you can search for it. See *Folksonomy*.

Turing test   A model used to prove whether a machine can be considered intelligent. In the blind test, a questioner is connected to two subjects, one human and one a machine. The questioner does not know which is which, but asks the same questions of both. If the machine can convince the questioner that it is human, it is considered intelligent. In 1990, Hugh Loebner offered a $100,000 prize to the maker of the first computer to pass the test.

Typosquatter An opportunistic marketer who takes advantage of misspelled words, such as adding an extra *r* to a trademark word with double *rr*'s. The typosquatter then tries to sell another, sometimes competing, product. For example, a carrot farmer may own that name and use it to market carrots. A typosquatter may use *carrrot* to sell a competing brand, to sell a patent medicine based on carrots, or the like.

URL *Uniform Resource Locator*, or a string of characters used to represent and identify a page of information on the World Wide Web.

Viral marketing The *viral phenomenon* refers to marketing or advertising techniques that use social networks to increase brand awareness or sales much in the way that diseases or computer viruses spread. This can be hand to hand, mouth to mouth, or computer to computer via the Internet. Viral marketing nudges people to voluntarily pass along a marketing message. The message may take the form of video clips, interactive games, e-books, intriguing images, or even text messages.

It is claimed that a customer tells an average of 3 people about a product or service he or she likes, and 11 people about a product or service that he or she did not like. Viral marketing is based on this natural human behavior.

Virtual reality   A computer simulation of a created three-dimensional world, often complete with action, sound effects, and other enhancements.

VoIP   *Voice-over-Internet protocol* allows the transmission of voice via the Internet or other packet-switched networks. VoIP is sometimes used to refer to the actual transmission of voice rather than the protocol that makes it possible.

Walls   Social networking site Facebook first used a "wall" to log the scratchings of friends. Users subsequently have created more advanced versions of the original wall, such as the application SuperWall.

Web 2.0   A term used to describe an evolving generation of a participatory Web. Web 2.0 describes the proliferation of interconnectivity and social interaction on the World Wide Web.

Webcam   Abbreviation of *Web camera*, a small camera that sends images through a computer for access on the Internet or instant messaging.

Web feed   Standardized protocols that allow end-users to make use of a site's data in a different context.

Wikis   A collection of Web pages that enables anyone who accesses them to contribute or modify content, using a simplified computer language.

Notes

INTRODUCTION

1. Gareth Mason, "High Resolution Google Satellite Launched," *World of Tech*, September 8, 2008.
2. "Google Rides Internet Ad Wave," Associated Press, October 18, 2007.
3. Tim Alton, "Have You Explored All the Wonders of Google?" *Indianapolis Business Journal*, April 2, 2007, p. 36.
4. Mark Malseed, "The Story of Sergey Brin: How the Moscow-Born Entrepreneur Cofounded Google—and Changed the Way the World Searches," *Moment*, February 20, 2007, p. 38.
5. Ken Auletta, "Search and Destroy," *New Yorker*, January 14, 2008.
6. Norman Douglas, *South Wind* (London: Pino Orioli, 1917).
7. "NASA Takes Google on a Journey into Space," Google website, www.Google.com/press, September 28, 2005.
8. Patrick Thibodeau, "Pentagon Looks to UPS, FedEx, Others for IT Advice," *ComputerWorld*, July 28, 2008.
9. Van Zanten, BorisVeldhuijzen, TheNextWeb.com, May 12, 2008.
10. David Smith, "The Observer," *The Guardian*, August 17, 2008.
11. Amy Schatz, "Google Will Offer Services for Bloggers at the Conventions," *Wall Street Journal*, August 19, 2008.
12. Adi Ignatius, "In Search of the Real Google," *Time*, February 20, 2006.
13. "Google, Apple Scores Rise in Customer Satisfaction Index," *East Bay Business Times*, August 19, 2006.

THE GOOGLE GUYS

1. Adi Ignatius, "In Search of the Real Google," *Time*, February 20, 2006.
2. Mark Malseed, "The Story of Sergey Brin: How the Moscow-Born Entrepreneur Cofounded Google and Changed the Way the World Searches," *Moment*, February 20, 2007, p. 38.
3. Virginia Scott, *Google: Corporations That Changed the World* (Westwood, CT: Greenwood Publishing Group, 2008).
4. Ibid.
5. Mark Malseed, "The Story of Sergey Brin," p. 45.
6. Ibid.
7. Michael Brin, University of Maryland profile of Sergey Brin.
8. Mark Malseed, "The Story of Sergey Brin," p. 46.
9. Ibid., p. 38.
10. Sergey Brin's blog, Too.blogspot.com.
11. Sergey Brin's personal blog.
12. University of Maryland website.
13. *The Oprah Winfrey Show*, November 18, 2008.
14. Author's conversation with Warren Buffett, December 15, 2008.
15. Mark Malseed, "The Story of Sergey Brin," p. 38.
16. Adi Ignatius, "In Search of the Real Google."
17. "Google Founders Have Grown Up," Reuters, May 9, 2008.
18. Mark Malseed, "The Story of Sergey Brin," p. 38.
19. Ibid., p. 38.
20. Verne Kopytoff, "Larry Page's Connections," *San Francisco Chronicle*, December 31, 2000.
21. From *The Google Story* by David A. Vise and Mark Malseed, copyright © 2005, by David A. Vise. Used by permission of Dell Publishing, a division of Random House, Inc.
22. www.Montessori-ami.org.
23. Ibid.
24. Ibid.
25. www.eecs.umich.edu/eecs/alumni/Stories/Page.html.
26. Ibid.
27. Barbara Palmer, "Following Creative Paths Both 'Circuitous and Serendipitous,'" *Stanford Report*, September 28, 2005.

28. From *The Google Story* by David A. Vise and Mark Malseed, copyright © 2005, by David A. Vise. Used by permission of Dell Publishing, a division of Random House, Inc.

29. Vern Kopytoff, "Larry Page's Connections."

30. Consumer Electronics Show (CES), Las Vegas, Nevada, January 6, 2006.

31. Jim Goldman, "Google's 'Oogle' of a Wedding," www.cnbc.com, November 15, 2007.

32. "Moon 2.0—NASA Projects Could Be Supported by a Commercial Transport and Delivery Network," www.news.com.au, October 31, 2008.

33. "Google Founders Have Grown Up."

34. From *The Google Story* by David A. Vise and Mark Malseed, copyright © 2005, by David A. Vise. Used by permission of Dell Publishing, a division of Random House, Inc.

35. Ibid., p. 29.

36. Randy Komisar of Kleiner, Perkins, Caulfield & Byers, Endeavor Entrepreneurs' Summit, Stanford University Entrepreneurship Corner.

37. "Jerry Yang and David Filo," Stanford University School of Engineering biography.

38. Shivanand Kanavi, "Mathematician at Heart," *Business India*, May 24–June 6, 2004.

39. From *The Google Story* by David A. Vise and Mark Malseed, copyright © 2005, by David A. Vise. Used by permission of Dell Publishing, a division of Random House, Inc.

40. John Battelle, *The Search: How Google and Its Rivals Rewrote the Rules of Business and Transformed Our Culture* (New York: Penguin Group, 2005), p. 68.

41. Ibid., p. 90.

42. Mark Malseed, "The Story of Sergey Brin," p. 47.

ADULT SUPERVISION

1. Eric Auchard, "Google Execs Pledge to Be Coworkers for Years," *Extreme Tech.com*, January 31, 2008.

2. Tim O'Reilly, "Web 2.0 Definition: Trying Again," radar.oreilly.com.archives, December 10, 2006.

3. Abbey Klaassen, "Talk about a Power Lunch," *Advertising Age*, October 15, 2007, p. 52.

4. Eric Schmidt, NASA 50th Anniversary Lecture, January 17, 2008.

5. "Google Founders Have Grown Up," Reuters, May 9, 2008.

6. First on CNBC: CNBC transcript: CNBC's Jim Cramer interviews Eric Schmidt, Google Chairman and CEO, on *Mad Money with Jim Cramer*, November 2, 2008.

7. Ibid.

8. "Eric Schmidt, Google's CEO, Qualifies as Mensch," *Denver Post,* Letter to the Editor from Nancy Litwack-Strong, Opinion section, November 9, 2008.

9. Eric Schmidt, NASA 50th Anniversary Lecture.

IN THE BEGINNING

1. From *The Google Story* by David A. Vise and Mark Malseed, copyright © 2005, by David A. Vise. Used by permission of Dell Publishing, a division of Random House, Inc.

2. Google Corporate Information, www.google.com/corporate/history/html.

3. Robert Colvile, "Google at Ten: How Did One Company Become Such a Part of Our Lives, So Fast?" *The Telegraph*, September 4, 2008.

4. From *The Google Story* by David A. Vise and Mark Malseed, copyright © 2005, by David A. Vise. Used by permission of Dell Publishing, a division of Random House, Inc.

5. Yuval Sa'ar, "The Israeli Woman behind the Google Logo," www.haaretz.com, February 11, 2008.

6. "AOL May Become Object of Microsoft, Yahoo!, Google's Desires," CNNMoney.com, July 21, 2008.

7. Marissa Mayer, Google blog, September, 12, 2008, www.google.com.

8. "Microsoft CEO: No Interest in Buying Yahoo!," Associated Press, Sydney, Australia, November 7, 2008.

9. Jefferson Graham, "The House that Helped Build Google," *USA Today*, July 4, 2007.

10. "Science as Inspiration," speech by Larry Page, Entrepreneur Thought Leader Speakers, YouTube, May 1, 2002.
11. http://www.wired.com/wired/archive/12.03, google_pr.html.
12. "Alumni Who've Made a Difference: Larry Page," EECS Almuni Stories, www.eecs.umich.edu.
13. Google Corporate Information, www.google.com/corporate/history/html.
14. Ibid.
15. Shivanand Kanvi, "Mathematician at Heart," *Business India*, May 24–June 6, 2004.
16. Interview with author, December 2008.
17. Larry page interview, Academy of Achievement, October 28, 2000, www.achievement.org.
18. Juan Carlos Perez, "Google, Microsoft, Facebook and MySpace Talk Platforms," IDG News Service, November 7, 2008.
19. Author interviews with Assistant Professor Joel West, San Jose State University, December 1–9, 2008.

GOOGLE BY ANY OTHER NAME

1. "How Google Got Its Colorful Logo," www.wired.com/rint/techbiz/startups/multimedia/2008/02/gallery.
2. Yuval Sa'ar, "The Israeli Woman behind the Google Logo," www.haaretz.com, February 11, 2008.
3. Ibid.
4. Emily Dugan, "Google Once Reviled Computer Superpowers but Domination Is Just What It Is Achieving," *The Independent*, September 7, 2008.
5. Conservatives website, "David Cameron: Speech to Google Zeitgeist Conference," October 12, 2007.

A COMPANY IS BORN

1. Sergey Brin, *Continuum* (alumni magazine), College of Computer, Mathematical & Physical Sciences, University of Maryland, 2003.
2. Shivanand Kanvi, "Mathematician at Heart," *Business India*, May 24–June 6, 2004.

3. "Jerry Yang and David Filo," Stanford University School of Engineering biography.

4. Jefferson Graham, "The House that Helped Build Google," *USA Today*, July 4, 2007.

5. John Battelle, *The Search: How Google and Its Rivals Rewrote the Rules of Business and Transformed Our Culture* (New York: Penguin Group, 2005), p. 89.

6. "John Doerr," John Battelle interview, www:battellemedia.com, November 20, 2007.

7. Laura Rich, "How John Doerr, the Old Professor, Finally Struck Google," *New York Times*, May 3, 2004.

8. Janet Driscoll Miller, "Why CRM Fails," www.marketingpilgrim.com, May 2007.

9. Ibid.

10. "Chaos as a Business Plan," *National Public Radio Marketplace*, Kai Ryssdal interview with Adam Lashinsky, September 26, 2006.

11. "U.S. Google Inc. to Join the World's Layoff Fad, Leaving 10,000 Contract Workers at Risk," *Taiwan News*, November 25, 2008.

12. Saul Hansell, "Google Wants to Dominate Madison Avenue, Too," *New York Times*, October 30, 2005.

13. John Batelle, "The Wizard of Ads: Google's Omid Kordestani Conjured a Formula that Took Its Sales to $3 Billion," *Time*, October 2005.

14. "AOL May Become Object of Microsoft, Yahoo!, Google's Desires," CNNMoney.com, July 21, 2008.

15. Ken Auletta, "Search and Destroy," *The New Yorker*, January 14, 2008, p. 30.

16. Matt Hartley and Grant Robertson, "Google@10," *The Globe and Mail*, September 6, 2008. Reprinted with permission of *The Globe and Mail*.

17. Jennifer Wells, "Google Conquers the Ad World One Plain-Text Blurb at a Time," *The Globe and Mail*, November 7, 2008. Reprinted with permission of *The Globe and Mail*.

18. Peter Whoriskey, "Advertisers Slow to Embrace Online Advertising," *Washington Post*, June 29, 2008.

19. Matt Hartley and Grant Robertson, "Google@10," *The Globe and Mail*, September 6, 2008. Reprinted with permission of *The Globe and Mail*.

20. Robert Colville, "Google at Ten: How Did One Company Become Such a Part of Our Lives, So Fast?" *The Telegraph*, September 4, 2008.

21. Jennifer Wells, "Google Conquers the Ad World One Plain-Text Blurb at a Time," *The Globe and Mail*, November 7, 2008. Reprinted with permission of *The Globe and Mail*.

22. From *The Google Story* by David A. Vise and Mark Malseed, copyright © 2005, by David A. Vise. Used by permission of Dell Publishing, a division of Random House, Inc.

23. Ibid.

24. John Battelle, *The Search*, p. 128.

25. Ken Belson, "Attending to the Needs of the Too Busy," *New York Times*, September 30, 2008.

26. Ibid.

GOING PUBLIC

1. Michael Malone, "Googlemania!" *Wired*, December 2003.

2. Ibid.

3. Jason Kottke, "Playboy Interview: Google Guys," *Playboy,* September 24, 2004.

4. Letter from the founders, "An Owner's Manual for Google's Shareholders," from the S1 Registration Statement with the Securities and Exchange Commission. Available from several sources including www.Google.com.

5. *Mad Money*, CNBC, August 12, 2008.

6. From *The Google Story* by David A. Vise and Mark Malseed, copyright © 2005, by David A. Vise. Used by Permission of Dell Publishing, a division of Random House, Inc.

7. Ibid.

8. Letter from the Founders, "An Owner's Manual for Google's Shareholders," from the S1 Registration Statement with the Securities and Exchange Commission, and from other sources, including Google.com.

9. Google's S1 Registration Statement to the SEC, April 29, 2004.

10. Allan Sloan, "Going Public May Be Google's First Bad Move," *Newsweek*, May 4, 2004, p. E03.

11. From *The Google Story* by David A. Vise and Mark Malseed, copyright © 2005, by David A. Vise. Used by permission of Dell Publishing, a division of Random House, Inc.

12. Alyce Lomax, "Google at 10: The Awkward Phase," *The Motley Fool*, Fool.com, September 9, 2008.

13. "Google Co-founder Says Penny-Pinchers Fuel Results," Reuters, October 17, 2008.

14. Ibid.

15. Jessica E. Vascellaro and Scott Morrison, "Google Gears Down for Tougher Times," *Wall Street Journal,* December 3, 2008, p. A1.

16. Linda Rosencrance, "Google Gets 70% of U.S. Searches," *Computer World*, July 20, 2008.

17. Alyce Lomax, "A More Frugal Google," *The Motley Fool*, Fool.com, December 2008.

THE VISION

1. Google Annual Report, Letter to Shareholders, 2004.

2. Robert Hof, "Google's Mayer: Staying Innovative in a Downturn," *BusinessWeek*, December 14, 2008.

3. http://www.wired.com/wired/archive/12.03, google_pr.html.

4. Virginia Scott, *Google: Corporations That Changed the World* (Westwood, CT: Greenwood Publishing Group, 2008).

5. Kai Rysdal interview, "Are You Feeling Lucky? Google Is," *National Public Radio Marketplace*, November 19, 2007.

6. Eric Schmidt in conversation with Ken Auletta, San Francisco, June 11, 2008.

7. Ken Auletta, "Search and Destroy," *The New Yorker*, January 14, 2008, p. 30.

8. "Enlightenment Man," *The Economist,* December 4, 2008.

9. Ken Auletta, "Search and Destroy," p. 30.

10. Stephen Shankland, "Google's Translation Center: Language Lessons for the Googlebot?" news.cnet.com/8301-1023.

11. Anick Jesdanun, "An Un-American Feel Aids Expanding U.S. Web Firms," Associated Press, New York, July 27, 2008.
12. Google Annual Report, Letter to Shareholders, 2007.
13. Anick Jesdanun, "An Un-American Feel Aids Expanding U.S. Web Firms."
14. Google Annual Report, Letter to Shareholders, 2007.
15. http://www.wired.com/wired/archive/12.03, google_pr.html.
16. John Jurgensen, "The Family Guy Goes On Line," *Wall Street Journal Weekend Journal,* September 5, 2008, p. W1.
17. Google Annual Report, Letter to Shareholders, 2005.
18. Adi Ignatius, "Meet the Google Guys," *Time,* February 20, 2006.
19. www.Google.com/corporate.
20. Frequently quoted.
21. Jason Kottke, "Playboy Interview: Google Guys," *Playboy,* September 24, 2004.
22. "Web 2.0 Summit: Entrepreneurial Spirit Too Strong for Google Alumni: The Money Was Great . . . Larry and Sergey Were Focused . . . But a Panel of Ex-Googlers Revealed Why They Have Now Gone Off to Build Their Own Web 2.0 Fortunes," *Information Week,* October 20, 2007.
23. Ibid.
24. Jason Kottke, "Playboy Interview: Google Guys."
25. Adam L. Penenberg, "Is Google Evil? It Knows More than the National Agency Ever Will. And Don't Assume for a Minute that It Can Keep a Secret," *Mother Jones,* November–December 2006, p. 67.
26. Ibid.
27. Mysearchgurublog.com, November 25, 2008.
28. http://xooglers.blogspot.com, posted February 19, 2007.
29. John Battelle, *The Search,* p. 139.
30. Eric Schmidt in conversation with Ken Auletta, San Francisco, June 11, 2008.
31. Seth Finkelstein, "Jew Watch, Google, and Search Engine Optimization," sethf.com/anticensorware/google/jew-watch.php.
32. www.google.com/explanation.html.
33. http://sethf.com/anticensorware/google/jew-watch.php.

34. http:/google-watch.org.
35. Eric Schmidt in conversation with Ken Auletta, San Francisco, June 11, 2008.

GOOGLE CULTURE

1. Frequently quoted.
2. Stephanie Olsen, "Newsmakers: Google's Man Behind the Curtain," CNET News.com, May 10, 2004.
3. Adam Lashinsky, "Back2Back Champs," *Fortune*, February 4, 2008, p. 70.
4. Letter from the Founders, "An Owner's Manual for Google's Shareholders," from the S1 Registration Statement with the Securities and Exchange Commission, and from other sources, including Google.com, 2004.
5. Eric Schmidt in conversation with Ken Auletta, San Francisco, June 11, 2008.
6. "Web 2.0 Summit: Entrepreneurial Spirit Too Strong for Google Alumni: The Money Was Great . . . Larry and Sergey Were Focused . . . But a Panel of Ex-Googlers Revealed Why They Have Now Gone Off to Build Their Own Web 2.0 Fortunes," *InformationWeek*, October 20, 2007.
7. Ken Auletta, "Search and Destroy," *The New Yorker*, January 14, 2008, p. 30.
8. Ibid.
9. Jeremy Caplan, "Google's Chief Looks Ahead," *Managing Growth*, October 2, 2006.
10. Ibid.
11. "Web 2.0 Summit: Entrepreneurial Spirit Too Strong for Google Alumni."
12. From an interview by the author, summer, 2008, with employee who wished to remain anonymous.
13. Chris Anderson, *The Long Tail* (New York: Hyperion, 2006).
14. Letter from the Founders, "An Owner's Manual for Google's Shareholders."
15. Elizabeth Montalbano, "Growing Pains for Google," *ComputerWorld*, October 20, 2008.

16. Jessica E. Vascellaro and Scott Morrison, "Google Gears Down for Tougher Times," *Wall Street Journal,* December 3, 2008.
17. Sewell Chan, "Google Transit Expands to New York," http://cityroom.blogs.nytimes.com/2008/09/23.
18. Matt Hartley and Grant Robertson, "Google@10," *The Globe and Mail*, September 6, 2008.
19. Tricia McDermott, "Defining Google," CBS News, January 2, 2005.
20. Adam Lashinsky, "Back2Back Champs," p. 70.
21. Ibid.; Verne Kopytoff, "Larry Page's Connections," *San Francisco Chronicle*, December 31, 2000.
22. Adam Lashinsky, "Back2Back Champs," p. 70.
23. http://features.blogs.fortune.cnn.com/2008/01/21/100-best-companies-to-work-for/.
24. Ibid.
25. Daniel DeBolt, "City of Google: In Coming Years, Internet Giant Could Triple Its Already Huge Amount of Office Space," *Mountain View Voice*, July 20, 2007.
26. Mark Malseed, "The Story of Sergey Brin: How the Moscow-Born Entrepreneur Cofounded Google and Changed the Way the World Searches," *Moment Magazine*, February 2007, p. 38.
27. Vasanth Sridharan, "Google's Ginormous Free Food Budget: $7,530 per Googler, $72 Million a Year," *Silicon Alley Insiders*, http://www.alleyinsider.com, April 23, 2008.
28. Dan Farber, "Kai Fu Lee: I Need to Follow My Heart," www.blogs.zdnet.com, August 9, 2005.
29. Letter from the Founders, "An Owner's Manual for Google's Shareholders."
30. John Batelle, "The Wizard of Ads: Google's Omid Kordestani Conjured a Formula that Took Its Sales to $3 Billion," *Time*, October 2005.
31. Wendy McLellan, "Google Targeting Talent with Innovative, Creative Qualities," Canwest News Service, July 28, 2008.
32. Ibid.
33. Google Labs Aptitude Test, *Linux Journal*, September 1, 2004.
34. Letter from the Founders, Initial Public Offering Registration Statement S1, 2004.
35. Quentin Hardy, "Close to the Vest," *Forbes,* July 2, 2007.

36. Dan Fost, "Keeping It All in the Google Family," *New York Times*, November 13, 2008.

37. Stephen E. Arnold, "The Summer of Transparency," *KM World*, August 31, 2008, www.kmworld.com.

38. Letter to Shareholders, Google S1 Public Offering Registration, 2004.

39. Daniel DeBolt, "City of Google."

40. "Google's Wall of Silence," Opinion page, *Mountain View Voice*, July 27, 2007.

41. Ibid.

42. Ibid.

43. Stephen E. Arnold, "The Summer of Transparency."

GOOGLE GROWS UP

1. Kevin Kelleher, "Who's Afraid of Google? Everyone," *Wired*, November 30, 2005.

2. "Google Founders Have Grown Up," Reuters, May 9, 2008.

3. Author interviews with Assistant Professor Joel West, San Jose State University, December 1–9, 2008.

4. From *The Google Story* by David A. Vise and Mark Malseed, copyright © 2005, by David A. Vise. Used by permission of Dell Publishing, a division of Random House, Inc.

5. Chris Kraeuter and Rachel Rosmarin, "Why Google Won't Give In," *Forbes*, January 24, 2006.

6. Ibid.

7. Ibid.

8. James Kirkup and Nicole Martin, "YouTube Attacked by MPs Over Sex and Violence Footage," *The Telegraph*, July 3, 2008.

9. Google corporate website, www.google.com.

10. Declan McCullagh, "Report Criticizes Google's Porn Filters," CNet News, News.cnet.com, April 10, 2003.

11. Matt Hartley and Grant Robertson, "Google@10," *The Globe and Mail*, September 6, 2008. Reprinted with permission of *The Globe and Mail*.

12. Abbey Klaassen, "Talk about a Power Lunch," *Advertising Age*, October 15, 2007, p. 52.

13. "Google Under Fire for 'Breathtaking' Hypocrisy, New Report Shows Just How Much Personal Information Is Available through Google Street View," *Marketwatch*, July 31, 2008.

14. Ibid.

15. Drake Bennett, "Stopping Google," *Boston Globe*, June 30, 2008, www.Boston.com.

16. Michael Dinan, "Privacy Issues, Government Probe Stir Hard Feelings between AT&T, Google," TMCnet, www.tmcnet.com, August 15, 2008.

17. Julia Bonstein, Marcel Rosenbach, and Hilmar Schmundt, "Data Mining You to Death," www.spiegel.de/international/germany, October 30, 2008. © 2008, Spiegel Online. Reprinted by permission.

18. Ibid.

19. Ibid.

20. John Letzing, "Web Firms Tread Carefully in Behavior Tracking," MarketWatch, September 10, 2008.

21. Lettter to Shareholders, Google 2005 Annual Report.

22. Emilie Dugan, "Google Once Reviled Computer Superpowers But Domination Is Just What It Is Achieving," *The Independent*, September 7, 2008.

23. Zusha Elinson, "Boring Couple Sues Google for Street View," *The Recorder*, April 9, 2008.

24. "Restatement of Torts," American Law Institute legal guideline; Cade Metz, "Google: Even in the Desert, Privacy Does Not Exist," www.theregister.co.uk, July 31, 2008.

25. Julia Bonstein, Marcel Rosenbach, and Hilmar Schmundt, "Data Mining You to Death."

26. Yoko Kubota, "Japanese Group Asks Google to Stop Map Service," Reuters, December 19, 2008.

27. Elinor Mills, "Google Balances Privacy, Reach," *CNET News*, July 14, 2005.

28. Eric Schmidt in conversation with Ken Auletta, San Francisco, June 11, 2008.

29. Drake Bennett, "Stopping Google," *Boston Globe*, June 30, 2008, www.Boston.com.

30. Ibid.

31. Ellen Nakashima, "Web Firms Acknowledge Tracking Behavior without Consent," *Los Angeles Times*, August 12, 2008.

32. Chris Williams, "Berlusconi Plans to Use G8 Presidency to 'Regulate the Internet,'" *The Register* (UK), December 3, 2008.

33. David Smith, "The Observer," *The Guardian*, August 17, 2008.

34. Adam L. Penenberg, "Is Google Evil? It Knows More than the National Agency Ever Will. And Don't Assume for a Minute that It Can Keep a Secret," *Mother Jones*, November–December 2006, p. 67.

35. Ken Auletta, "Search and Destroy," *The New Yorker*, January 14, 2008, p. 30.

36. Thomas Claburn, "Google Told to Reveal Gmail 'Spybox' Account Info in CTO Espionage Case," *InformationWeek*, October 20, 2008.

37. Ibid.

38. Vint Cerf, "The Internet is for Everyone," Memo to the Internet Society, April, 2002.

39. Janine Zacharia, "Google Inc. Navigates Foreign Laws," Bloomberg News, June 6, 2008.

40. "Google Committed to Staying in China," *PC Magazine*, June 9, 2006.

41. David Smith, "Google Defiant Over Censorship in China," *The Observer*, October 29, 2006.

42. "Google Committed to Staying in China."

43. Microsoft news release, October 29, 2008.

44. Ibid.

45. Roy Blount Jr., "$125 Million Settlement in *Authors Guild v. Google*," www.authorsguild.org/advocacy, October 28, 2008.

46. Jonathan V. Last, "Google and Its Enemies: The Much-Hyped Project to Digitize 32 Million Books Sounds Like a Good Idea. Why Are So Many People Taking Shots at It?" *Weekly Standard*, December 10, 2007.

47. Ibid.

48. Jefferson Graham, "Google to Sell Books to Be Read Only Online," *USA Today*, October 29, 208.

49. From Google's website, The Library Project.

50. Jonathan V. Last, "Google and Its Enemies."

51. Ken Auletta, "Search and Destroy."

52. Robin Jeweler, "The Google Book Search Project: Is Online Indexing a Fair Use Under Copyright Law?" Congressional Research Services (CRS) Reports and Issue Briefs, December 2005.

53. "More Digitized Books on Internet as Google Settles Lawsuit," www.enews20.com, October 28, 2008.

54. Ibid.

55. Reyhan Harmanci, "Google, Book Trade Groups Settle Lawsuits," *San Francisco Chronicle*, October 29, 2008, p. C-1.

56. http://jobline.acc.com, "Google Legal Opportunities."

57. Emily Steel, "Google Search Ads Rile Its Big Customers," *Wall Street Journal*, June 4, 2008.

58. Ibid.

59. "Google Says Viacom Lawsuit a Threat to Internet Users," Reuters, May 1, 2007.

60. Kenneth Li, "Google Takes a Swipe at Viacom," Reuters, July 13, 2007.

61. "Mediaset Sues Google, YouTube; Seeks $780 million," Reuters, July 30, 2008.

62. Knol, Google's information source: "Google Ordered to Reveal Blogger Identity in Defamation Suit in India."

63. Steven Ellis, "High Court to Rule on Age Discrimination Suit Against Google," *Metropolitan News-Enterprise*, January 31, 2008.

64. John Battelle, *The Search: How Google and Its Rivals Rewrote the Rules of Business and Transformed Our Culture* (New York: Penguin Group, 2005), p. 234.

65. The Packet Rat, "Net Neutrality Doesn't Get Google's First-Class Treatment," *Government Computer News*, July 24, 2006.

66. Ibid.

67. Corporate website, www.google.com.

68. Ibid.

GOOD CITIZEN GOOGLE

1. First on CNBC: CNBC transcript: CNBC's Jim Cramer interviews Eric Schmidt, Google Chairman and CEO on *Mad Money with Jim Cramer*, Friday, November 7, 2008.

2. John Reid Blackwell, "Google Chief: Invest in Energy Independence: Schmidt Urges Focus on Wind, Solar, Other Renewable Sources," *Richmond Times-Dispatch*, October 31, 2008.

3. Joe Truini, "Feeling Lucky: Google to Spend Tens of Millions on Green Energy," *Waste News*, December 10, 2007, p. 1.

4. Stephen Shankland, "Google Execs Cheery about Silicon Valley Economy," http://news.cnet.com/, September 18, 2008.

5. "Google to Spend Millions to Develop Renewable Energy Business: Google's Goal Is to Work with Other Developing Technologies that Can Harness Solar, Geothermal, Wind, or Other Renewable Energy Sources," *Information Week*, November 27, 2007.

6. Jim Offner, "After Their Tech Empires Are Built," *E-Commerce Times*, November 20, 2008.

7. Stephen Shankland, "Google Execs Cheery about Silicon Valley Economy."

8. Joe Truini, "Feeling Lucky," p. 1.

9. "Google to Spend Millions to Develop Renewable Energy Business."

GOOGLE'S FUTURE

1. Stephen E. Arnold, "The Summer of Transparency," *KM World*, www.kmworld.com, August 31, 2008.

2. Elizabeth Motalbano, "Growing Pains for Google," *ComputerWorld*, October 20, 2008.

3. Ken Auletta, "Search and Destroy," *The New Yorker*, January 14, 2008, p. 30.

4. www.google.com/corporate/history.html.

5. Chris Taylor, "Imagining the Google Future: Top Experts Help Us Plot Four Scenarios that Show Where the Company's Geniuses May Be Leading It . . . and Perhaps All of Us," Business 2.0, *Time*, January–February 2006.

6. www.skynews.com, September 5, 2008.

7. Eric Schmidt in conversation with Ken Auletta, San Francisco, June 11, 2008.

8. Nicholas Carlson, "RIP Google Good Times: Slowing Hiring, Deals and Travel," www.alleyinsider.com, October 21, 2008.

9. Michael Liedtke, "Google Stock Soars on 26 pct Jump in 3Q Earnings," AP Business Writer, November 14, 2008.

10. Ibid.

11. Prabudev Konana, "Sensible Capitalism Needed," *The Hindu*, December 2, 2008.

12. Saul Hansell, "Google Wants to Dominate Madison Avenue, Too," *New York Times,* October 30, 2005.

13. Larry Page, speaking at the American Association for the Advancement of Science, San Francisco, www.blogoscope.com, February 16, 2007.

14. Ibid.

15. Saul Hansell, "Google Wants to Dominate Madison Avenue, Too."

16. http://www.youtube.com/user/IgnoranceIsntBliss, October 28, 2000.

17. www.law.com/jsp/legaltechnology/pubArticleLT, August 20, 2007.

18. Andy Greenberg, "Google Grows Up," *BusinessWeek,* January 11, 2008.

19. Ibid.

20. Jaso Szep, "Technology Reshapes America's Classrooms," Reuters, July 7, 2008.

21. Gregory M. Lamb, "With New Web Services, More Companies Are Working in the 'Cloud,'" www.features.csmonitor.com/innovation, November 11, 2008.

22. "Technology Will Continue to Drive the Working Lives of Young People," *Kalamazoo Gazette*, www.kzgazette/2008/06/google, June 4, 2008.

23. Ibid.

24. Jaso Szep, "Technology Reshapes America's Classrooms."

25. Jeremy Caplan, "Google's Chief Looks Ahead," *Time*, October 2, 2006.

26. Gregory M. Lamb, "With New Web Services, More Companies Are Working in the 'Cloud.'"

27. Tim O'Reilly, "My Commencement Speech at SIMS," *O'Reilly Radar,* http://radar.oreilly.com, May 14, 2006.

28. Google Inc., Form S1 Registration Statement, Securities and Exchange Commission, April 29, 2004, p. 15.

29. *Mad Money*, CNBC, August 13, 2008.

30. Lawrence Donegan, "YouTube Live: Stars of Online Video Take a Real World Bow," *The Guardian*, November 24, 2008.

31. Michael Liedtke, "YouTube Flips Switch on New Sales Channel," Associated Press, October 6, 2008.

32. John Battelle interview with Eric Schmidt, Web 2.0 Expo, April 17, 2007.

33. www.google.com.

34. Betsy Schiffman, "Eric Schmidt: Google Mission Is to 'Change the World,'" Wired.com, June 11, 2008.

35. From the Official Google Blog, "The First Android-Powered Phone," Ackerman, September 23, 2008.

36. Elise Ackerman, "Look Out I, Here's G," *San Jose Mercury News*, September 24, 2008.

37. Juan Carlos Perez, "Google Releases Android SDK," *Australian PC World*, Summer 2008, p. 16.

38. *New York Times* weblog, June 23, 2008.

39. Leslie Cauley, "Google Vaults into Global Wireless Ring with G1 Phone," *USA Today*, September 24, 2008, p. 3B.

40. Marguerite Reardon, "FCC Opens Free 'White Space' Spectrum," CNET News, News.cnet.com, November 4, 2008.

41. Nate Anderson, "Google White Space Petition: 13,000 Signatures and Counting," Arstechnica.com/news, September 2, 2008.

42. Wireless Communications Association Conference, San Jose, November 6, 2008.

43. Andrew LaVallee, "A Second Look at Citiwide Wi-Fi," *Wall Street Journal*," December 8, 2008.

44. Larry Page, Google's White Space Blog, and IDG News Service, November 5, 2008.

THE DOMINANT POWER IN THE INDUSTRY?

1. Robert Hof, "Is Google Too Powerful?" *BusinessWeek*, April 9, 2007.

2. David Smith, "The Observer," *The Guardian*, August 17, 2008.

3. Matt Hartley and Grant Robertson, "Google@10," *The Globe and Mail*, September 6, 2008. Reprinted with permission of *The Globe and Mail.*

4. Ben Oliver, "The Battery-Powered Supercar that's Electrifying the World," www.dailymail.co.uk, November 11, 2008.

5. Robert Hof, "Is Google Too Powerful?"

6. Esther Dyson, "Google Meets Its Motto—for Now," *Taipai Times*, December 22, 2008, p. 9.

7. Ken Auletta, "The Search Party," *New Yorker*, January 14, 2008.

8. Robert Hof, "Google's Mayer: Staying Innovative in a Downturn," *BusinessWeek*, December 14, 2008.

9. Esther Dyson, "Google Meets Its Motto—for Now."

10. Josh Reynolds, "Google, eBay Battling Over Payment Service," Associated Press, June 15, 2007.

11. Ibid.

12. Ibid.

13. Matt Hartley and Grant Robertson, "Google@10."

14. Jeremy Caplan, "Google's Chief Looks Ahead," *Time,* October 2, 2006.

15. Elinor Mills, "Microsoft Won't Make a Netscape of Us," CNET News, May 11, 2006.

16. From *The Google Story* by David A. Vise and Mark Malseed, copyright © 2005, by David A. Vise. Used by permission of Dell Publishing, a division of Random House, Inc.

17. *Mad Money*, CNBC, August 12, 2008.

18. Terry McCrann, "Rupert Murdoch's New World Order," *Herald Sun* (Australia), November 1, 2008.

19. http://www.wired.com/wired/archive/12.03, google_pr.html.

20. Jeffrey Herron, "Schmidt: Independent Yahoo! Better for Competition," Associated Press, June 12, 2008.

21. Ibid.

22. Richard Waters, "Why Google Should Heed the DoJ's Wake-up Call," blogs.ft.com/techblog/2008, November 5, 2008.

23. "Google Bails Out of Yahoo! Ad Deal," AOL Money & Finance, money.aol.com/news, November 5, 2008.

24. "Microsoft CEO: No Interest in Buying Yahoo!," Associated Press, Sydney, Australia, November 7, 2008.

25. David Lyons, "Tough Customers," *Forbes Global*, April 7, 2008, p. 69.

26. Clayton Harrison, "Yahoo!'s Yang Faces Sagging Profit After Icahn Row," Bloomberg.com, July 22, 2008.

27. Michael Helft, "Google Ends Microsoft's Yahoo! Search," *New York Times*, May 6, 2008.

28. Jason Kottke, "Playboy Interview: Google Guys," *Playboy*, September 24, 2004.

29. David A. Vise and Mark Malseed, *The Google Story*, p. 250.

30. Discussion between author and Bill Gates, Berkshire Hathaway annual meeting, May 2, 2008.

31. Adam L. Penenberg, "Is Google Evil? It Knows More than the National Agency Ever Will. And Don't Assume for a Minute that It Can Keep a Secret," *Mother Jones*, November–December 2006, p. 67.

CONCLUSION

1. http://www.wired.com/wired/archive/12.03, google_pr.html.

2. Sergey Brin, Web 2.0 Conference, October 9, 2005.

3. Michael Liedtke, "Google Searches for Its Place in the Future," Associated Press, September 14, 2008.

4. Robert Hof, "Is Google Too Powerful?" *BusinessWeek*, April 9, 2007.

5. Matt Hartley and Grant Robertson, "Google@10," *The Globe and Mail*, September 6, 2008. Reprinted with permission of *The Globe and Mail*.

6. Chris O'Brien, "Invincible No More?" *San Jose Mercury News*, August 24, 2008, p. E1.

7. Stephen Shankland, "Google Execs Cheery about Silicon Valley Economy," http://news.cnet.com/, September 18, 2008.

8. Henry Blodget, "Google Sucks Life Out of Old Media: Check Out the 2007 Share Shift," *Alley Insider*, www.alleyinsider.com, March 14, 2008.

9. Ibid.

10. Michael Liedtke, "Google Searches for Its Place in the Future."

Permissions

Permission has been granted by the following organizations and individuals for quotes appearing in this book:

Ken Anletta
Business India
The Globe and Mail
KM World
Playboy Magazine
Random House
Spiegel Online